WALT DISNEY WORLD HIDDEN HISTORY

Remnants of Former Attractions and Other Tributes

Kevin Yee

Ultimate Orlando Press
Orlando, Florida

Walt Disney World Hidden History: Remnants of Former Attractions and
Other Tributes
by Kevin Yee

Published by
ULTIMATE ORLANDO PRESS
www.ultimateorlando.com

Cover design by Kwok Yin Mak

ISBN-13: 978-0-9831599-0-2

FIRST EDITION
2010 Printing
Printed in the United States of America

To Michelle

No book is written alone. This one came into being with the patient help of numerous sources, readers, and friends, among them Tony Baxter, Bruce Gordon, Joe Lanzisero, Kim Irvine, Doug Hartwell, Bob Baranick, Eddie Sotto, Bob Gurr, Chris Merritt, Josh Shipley, Bill Watkins, Jim Korkis, Lonnie Hicks, Duncan Dickson, Reed Cunningham, John Frost, Eric Main, Doobie and Rebekah Moseley, Jeff Lange, Denise Preskitt, Matt Heitzmann, Dan Morrow, and Jorge Morales. My coauthor on the Disneyland books, Jason Schultz, was invaluable in the early research process for this book as well.

Enormous thanks go to my early test readers Jeff Carter, Larisa Smith, Katie and David Carver, Douglas Quintanilla, Heather Werth, David R. Axmann, and Kevin and Kelly Lusk. They saved me from myself on innumerable occasions. Any typos that remain are not their fault, but mine.

Finally, I want to give thanks to my wife Michelle and sons Devon and Tyler for their patience and understanding during the genesis of this book. They enrich my life every day.

Table of Contents

Introduction

The constantly-evolving nature of Walt Disney World is part of its allure. Every year the theme parks reinvent and redefine themselves, often by introducing new attractions and replacing older ones. The designers of the attractions, called Imagineers (a coin termed by Walt Disney himself to merge both "imagination" and "engineers"), frequently show their reverence for "what came before" by re-using small reminders of former rides in newer ones.

These homages are scattered about like Easter eggs left for visitors to find, and are sometimes accompanied by other tributes: inside jokes about thematic elements, re-used figures and characters, even personal touches like the designers' own initials incorporated into thematic elements in the show. These tributes and inside references deposit layers of meaning and history to a form of entertainment often enjoyed on the strengths of its surface value alone. They impart ulterior significance to the attractions and the people who design them, and ultimately remind us why we found them so special in the first place.

The level of attention paid to even the least noticeable details helps impart to Walt Disney World its distinctive magic. Savoring the details will enrich the experience, no matter how often you visit.

Kevin Yee

Magic Kingdom

Wonders of Life Arch

The arch holding the "Magic Kingdom" sign at the parking lot booths for the Transportation and Ticket Center comes from the former Wonders of Life pavilion at Epcot. Before the pavilion was converted to seasonal use and employed as a festival center, it had this arch across its entry way.

Richard Irvine and Joe Potter

Together with Disney executive Richard Irvine, retired Army General Joe Potter was a central figure in the construction of Walt Disney World. Today, the primary ferries crossing the Seven Seas Lagoon are named after them. On the bottom level of each ferry, a large portrait and a brief biography of that ferry's namesake can be found.

Walt Disney's Window

Walt Disney is honored with a window directly on the train station, facing out toward the Main Entrance of the park.

Ticket Book Advertisements

Attraction posters in the tunnels under the train station are holdovers from the days when the Magic Kingdom used ticket books. Before the all-day passport debuted in 1980, patrons had to buy individual ride tickets, and the park therefore had an incentive to advertise lesser-traveled attractions.

Roy's Bench

A bench in Town Square honors Roy O. Disney, who opened Walt Disney World after his brother passed away in 1966. Walt Disney's role in the company's theme parks is obvious, and his tributes—such as the "Partners" statue with Mickey Mouse in the center of the Magic Kingdom— are equally hard to miss. But his brother Roy Disney was the one who lived to see Walt Disney World opened in 1971. He is honored in today's Magic Kingdom with a statue sitting on a bench in Town Square. The form and composition of Roy's statue are deliberate echoes of the more visible "Partners" statue of Walt with Mickey, and the statue of Roy posing with Minnie Mouse offers a bookend to Main Street.

Train Photos

Photographs below the Main Street Train Station honor The Walt Disney Company's long history with trains. Some of the pictures adorning the walls of the stroller rental area show the Magic Kingdom's locomotives as they existed in their former industrial lives, and other nearby photographs feature Walt Disney and the miniature backyard train at his Holmby Hills estate. One information board makes casual reference to former Santa Fe company executives, whose names are also used for the locomotives at Disneyland. A second board gives subtle tribute to Disney employee and fellow train enthusiast Ward Kimball. The board mentions Ward's personal full-sized train, which he dubbed Grizzly Flats, and had kept at his own property. Further signs explain how Walt's love of trains contributed to the idea that became Disneyland and the Magic Kingdom.

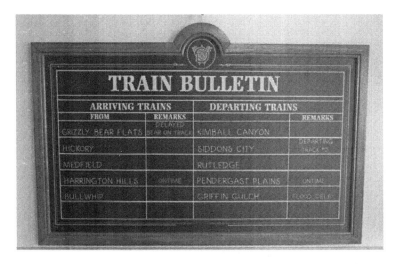

TRAIN BULLETIN

ARRIVING TRAINS		DEPARTING TRAINS	
FROM	REMARKS		REMARKS
GRIZZLY BEAR FLATS	DELAYED BEAR ON TRACK	KIMBALL CANYON	
HICKORY		GIDDONS CITY	DEPARTING TRACK #2
MEDFIELD		RUTLEDGE	
HARRINGTON HILLS	ON TIME	PENDERGAST PLAINS	ON TIME
BULLWHIP		GRIFFIN GULCH	FLOOD CELL

Magic Kingdom's Opening Year

The fire station on Main Street pays tribute to the year that the Magic Kingdom opened. Though above-ground construction started in 1969, the Magic Kingdom did not open until 1971. In honor of that year, the fire station purports to be "Engine Co. 71" in brass lettering visible high on the building's front side. Inside the station, a barrel makes another mention of Engine Company 71. A sign halfway up Main Street at one doorway near the Athletic Club also mentions that the "casting agency" has been open since '71. This doorway sign pays tribute to the Cast Members at Walt Disney World throughout the years.

Original Dapper Dans

A drawing on the wall of the Harmony Barber Shop shows the likeness of the original four Dapper Dans, the barbershop quartet which roams Main Street entertaining visitors. Since they got their start inside the barber shop, it seemed a logical place for a tribute.

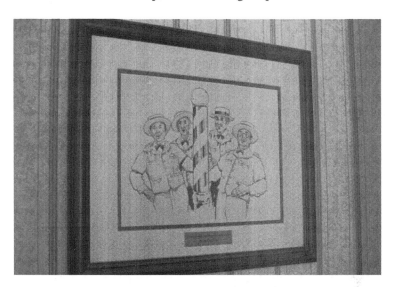

Turn of the Century America

Up the road, a sign above one doorway for the Emporium claims it was established in 1901—the year Walt Disney was born. A colorful mural near the ceiling just inside this section of the Emporium also mentions 1901. Main Street purports to be a sanitized version of a typical small American town circa 1890-1910, a period during which Walt was heavily influenced by his time spent as a child in the small town of Marceline, Missouri. Traces of this time frame are everywhere. For instance, gas lamps exist side by side with electric lights along the street, capturing the moment when America "went electric." Antique mutoscopes, which approximate a film by flipping through static pictures, entertain visitors at the Main Street train station. They were moved here when the Penny Arcade was converted to a shop, while other mutoscopes found homes at the

Boardwalk resort and the prop warehouse at Disney's Hollywood Studio's Backlot Tour.

Window Homages

Many of the windows along the second story of Main Street are decorated with the names of important individuals who made significant contributions to Walt Disney World. From General Joe Potter, the construction expert who oversaw the building of the Magic Kingdom, to Earl Vilmer, who renovated the Walt Disney World Railroad locomotives, these windows give credit to the often overlooked people whose years of hard work enabled the Magic Kingdom to thrive. At Disneyland, where the tradition of using such second-story windows to honor important company officials began, a majority of the people honored are artists and engineers (dubbed "Imagineers") who helped build and design that park. At the Magic Kingdom, there are more managers and administrators listed, such as the onetime head of Walt Disney World security, the chief Walt Disney World accountant, or the director of the Walt Disney World paint shop.

Walt Disney's Dentist

Thomas McCrumb, listed as the proprietor of the candy store on Main Street, was actually the personal dentist to a young Walt Disney (he once commissioned one of Walt's earliest films called *Tommy Tucker's Tooth*). The backstory of this store is that McCrumb visited the 1893 Chicago World's Fair (look for a certificate on the wall by the cashier to this effect), where he was so impressed by the gears and levers of machination that he added such automation to his own candy shop back on Main Street. There's even a further connection to that same world's fair: parts of it were built by Walt Disney's father Elias when he worked as a contractor. Unsurprisingly, elsewhere on Main Street, Elias Disney has his own window, where he is listed as a contractor.

Summer Magic

A 1963 movie called *Summer Magic* provided several songs for the background music heard on Main Street, but even more subtle tributes are found in the character names from the movie. Nancy and Julia, cousins in the film, are listed as the owners of Le Chapeau. Osh Popham, the general store owner in the movie, similarly runs the Emporium at Magic Kingdom. His name is stenciled on display windows facing Town Square diagonally.

Emporium Imagineers

One painted mural near the ceiling in the Emporium depicts the Imagineers who worked on the expansion of this shop, including Art Director Agnes David-Hoffman, Jim Heffron, Cicero Greathouse, and Katie Roser. Imagineer Joyce Carlson is also here, wearing the flowered hat in the bottom-left, though she did not work on the expansion of the Emporium.

Main Street Cinema

The ceiling of the Main Street Cinema contains a hexagonal box that once housed projectors. This store was once an actual cinema, showing several early Disney cartoons simultaneously on different screens on a looping basis. Multiple screens around the room were employed, and the projector box in the ceiling still shows evidence of where the projectors aimed. One of the projectors and one screen were preserved and kept in use when the cinema was replaced by the store in 1998. Because these cartoons had played in the park for so long, park managers wanted to continue to show them to the public, and one of the two Walt Disney Story theaters in Exposition Hall was refurbished for this purpose. Originally the cartoons were silent films, in keeping with the Main Street theme of a turn-of-the-century town. Synchronized sound hadn't been invented yet, nor had Mickey Mouse. Because the public kept asking for Mickey Mouse cartoons, several Mickey shorts were introduced in 1978, which is the year Mickey celebrated his 50th birthday.

Tobacconist Shop

The wooden Indian statue now in front of the Crystal Arts store is a remnant of a tobacconist shop that once sold tobacco products on Main Street. Originally, the statue served as an advertisement for the tobacco shop, when it was located across the street (near today's Hall of Champions). When the tobacco shop closed in 2000, the statue moved across the street to the Market House, which still sold cigarettes. Crystal Arts then expanded in 2006 to take over the Market House, and the Indian now sits as a reminder of what was once available. A duplicate statue can be found in Frontierland, where the thematic link to a general store is even stronger.

Market House

Items atop a display case in Crystal Arts are remnants of the former store in this space. The Crystal Arts store was originally a smaller shop. The space on the "corner" of Center Street was then not Crystal Arts, but the Market House, a representation of the general goods store common at the turn of the century. When Crystal Arts expanded here in 2006, the antique stove and most props were removed, but a few persisted atop display cases, like an antique typewriter and metal scales.

Shell Companies

Windows above the Crystal Arts store on Main Street list the names of the fake ("shell") companies used to buy the land Walt Disney World would be built upon. The forty-three square miles eventually purchased for Walt Disney World had to be bought from multiple owners who would have raised their asking price if they knew Disney was behind the acquisitions, so Walt used secrecy to hide his intentions. To make the purchases, he sent unknown emissaries that ostensibly operated for companies which turned out to not actually exist, including one "Ayefour Corporation" (a subtle reference to the nearby I-4 interstate freeway).

Walt's Window

Walt Disney is honored on a window above the Plaza Ice Cream
Parlor. Both Roy O. Disney and his son, Roy E. Disney, have
windows on Main Street that acknowledge their lasting influence on
the company. At Disneyland, Walt Disney didn't want a window
dedicated to himself, but when he died, park designers sought to
honor him in this fashion at Walt Disney World. Walt's window is
one of the few such tribute windows that face Cinderella Castle,
marking the location as a place of honor. This is actually Walt's
second window on Main Street. He has another highly visible
window at the railroad station, facing out toward the park's main
entrance. These two windows make it possible to consider all of
Main Street to be like the opening reel of a motion picture which
shows the production credits. If the windows on the buildings all
along the street give credit to those "behind the camera" making the
park come true, Walt's name appropriately comes both first and last,
as he is the director of the entire production. It is no coincidence
that most of the early Imagineers were artists from movie studios,
familiar primarily with storytelling and movie-style showmanship.
For this reason, Walt and his artists constructed visual "weenies" to
lure visitors to the next "reel" of the "motion picture," such as a
castle for Fantasyland or a tall white steamship for Frontierland.

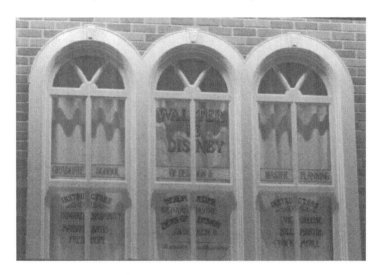

Casey's Corner Imagineers

One team photo on the wall of Casey's Corner is modern, and shows the Imagineers responsible for this restaurant's 1995 refurbishment... including some females, also shown wearing mustaches in the picture!

Plaza Swan Boats

An unused structure near the Central Plaza was once a loading dock for a boat ride. The Plaza Swan Boats circled the Central Plaza in the Magic Kingdom's early years, gliding along tracks at an automatically-controlled pace and offering a tranquil journey around the castle and its carefully manicured lawns. More of a relaxing atmosphere ride than a mode of transportation, the Swan Boats unfortunately suffered from low capacity and eventually succumbed to the march of time. Like the dock in Liberty Square once home to flat-bottomed keelboats that freely roamed the Rivers of America, the Swan Boat dock has no current function apart from serving as a reminder of the ride once housed here. The loading dock today may be little more than shelter from the elements, but the tracks still exist along the bottom of the moat around the Central Plaza. The front of the Swan Boats were shaped like giant white swans—a thematic nod to Disneyland's longstanding tradition of housing real swans in the moat around its castle. The pathway to the loading dock is still marked by topiary shrubs carefully groomed in the shape of swans.

The Best Time of Your Life

A song heard in the background musical loop at the Tomorrowland Terrace Noodle Station is an instrumental version of a now-defunct song from Carousel of Progress. From 1975-1993, the theme song of the attraction (which had undergone many changes and updates over the years) was "The Best Time of Your Life" rather than the original song "There's a Great Big Beautiful Tomorrow" (which returned to the attraction in 1993).

Walt's Future City

The model visible from the PeopleMover ride was created as the original vision of EPCOT. The first idea for EPCOT (which stood for Experimental Prototype Community of Tomorrow) was a revolutionary new kind of city planned to be built on Disney property. The model for it, now named Progress City, was created to show off Walt's concept. While this vision of EPCOT never materialized, part of the enormous model lives on in Tomorrowland. The dreams of a community of tomorrow do exist, in a fashion, in today's Tomorrowland. The land is themed to represent an intergalactic spaceport, with robots, aliens, and humans commingling in one peaceful society. While Tomorrowland in Disneyland Paris draws inspiration from Jules Verne, the Magic Kingdom's vision of the future is derived from Buck Rogers and Flash Gordon, with campy flying saucers serving as decorations throughout the land.

Flight to the Moon

One portion of the audio on the Tomorrowland Transit Authority PeopleMover honors a former attraction called Flight to the Moon. While traveling through Space Mountain on the PeopleMover, we hear terminal-style announcements saying: "Paging Mr. Morrow, Mr. Tom Morrow. Please contact Mr. Johnson in the control tower to confirm your flight to the moon"—a reference to the animatronic "host" of Flight to the Moon, also wittily named Tom Morrow. This attraction later become Mission to Mars, and then was replaced by Alien Encounter, which in turn gave way to Stitch's Great Escape. The Mr. Morrow animatronic in Mission to Mars was earlier referred to as "Mr. Johnson," so the announcement on the PeopleMover pays double tribute to the character. The general layout of Stitch's Great Escape, and the ExtraTERRORestrial Alien Encounter before it, can be traced directly to Mission to Mars and Flight to the Moon. In the original attraction, the preshow featured an interactive conversation with Mr. Morrow as he stood in the control room. Visitors then moved to one of two circular theaters set up to see viewscreens in the floor, ceiling, and sides of the theater, which captured the action as our rocket ship blasted off, made its way to Mars, and returned home. Today's attraction adds hardware, particularly in the center of the theater and in the interactive seat restraints, but the layout of rooms and even some of the viewscreens remain largely the same.

Alien Encounter

An Astro Orbiter vehicle alongside the PeopleMover was placed here because of a former Tomorrowland attraction. The Astro Orbiter vehicle visible just after the Progress City model contains an alien about to blast into space. This reference to Tomorrowland's status as a spaceport for aliens dates to 1994, when an attraction called the ExtraTERRORestrial Alien Encounter replaced Mission to Mars. On the occasion of its addition, the entire land was given a facelift and re-conceived as a spaceport. Today's Astro Orbiter replaced a similar ride called Star Jets, which featured a vehicle design with larger wings, as if necessary for planetary re-entry. Without Alien Encounter, Tomorrowland today might still be a disjointed celebration of futurism and space travel without a sense of a specific place like a spaceport.

Opening Date for Stitch's Great Escape

A plaque next to the entrance doors for Stitch's Great Escape may be written with letters that look alien, but they are really just stylized English letters. The plaque commemorates the opening date for the attraction. It reads: "Dedication. This Galactic Federation prisoner teleport center is hereby dedicated to the preservation of peace and harmony throughout the galaxy by protecting the nice from the naughty. The Grand Councilwomen [sic]. 2004 November 16."

Skippy

The second preshow room of Stitch's Great Escape features two teleportation tubes that show different aliens being transported to our location. In the Alien Encounter version of the show, these tubes were used to teleport a single cute critter named Skippy from one end of the room to the other, but a teleportation accident leaves him looking different on the other side. In the current show, the two animatronics are meant to represent completely different beings, but they were once the same character.

X-S Tech

One piece of futuristic equipment visible after the preshow for Stitch's Great Escape still bears the name of a fictional private company from Alien Encounter. The company, X-S Tech (an obvious pun on technology), featured heavily in Alien Encounter as the creator of the teleportation technology, but is not explicitly mentioned in Stitch's Great Escape. The machines with this logo can be seen on the right side of the path as visitors head toward the "Level Three" chamber to meet Stitch.

Alien Spaceport

Murals in the Merchant of Venus store call further attention to the alien spaceport concept. Designed to show off the rest of Tomorrowland as if the walls were transparent windows rather than paintings, these murals behind the cash registers show the familiar Tomorrowland architecture and depict Stitch-like aliens wandering about the land. Stitch is specifically referenced even outside the attraction to bear his name. One painted mural at the exit to Buzz Lightyear's Space Ranger Spin features a very small image of the spacecraft from the *Lilo and Stitch* movie. Sharp-eyed patrons will even notice Stitch's footprints on the ceiling of Merchant of Venus.

Timekeeper

The antenna dishes seen in the queue of Monster Inc. Laugh Floor are holdovers from the previous tenant here. The attraction which preceded Monsters Inc. Laugh Floor was a Circle-Vision movie called Timekeeper, which included an Audio-Animatronics host designed to look like a futuristic robot. Because the audience was time-traveling and the theme of Tomorrowland was one of a spaceport, many design elements emphasized interstellar commerce and communication. The antenna dishes in the Timekeeper queue made thematic sense then, but less so with the Monstropolis theme.

Circle-Vision 360

The curved back wall of the Monsters, Inc. Laugh Floor is a structural remnant of the original occupant here, the Circle-Vision 360 theater. Films such as *America the Beautiful* and *Magic Carpet 'Round the World* played here starting in 1971, and the Circle-Vision theater remained untouched for the Timekeeper replacement starting in 1994. The transition to the Monsters Inc. Laugh Floor brought many changes to the building's décor, but the circular shape of the main room was dictated by the building's fundamental structure, designed long ago for the Circle-Vision movies.

Dreamflight

A set piece in Buzz Lightyear's Space Ranger Spin is left unaltered from the previous attraction in this location. The rotating red light amid fog just prior to the theater-like finale of Buzz Lightyear is actually a remnant from the previous inhabitant, Dreamflight, which was also known as Take Flight for many years. This set was originally meant to signify our vehicles entering a giant turbine engine, as the ride was first sponsored by Eastern Airlines, then

Delta Airlines. The red frame overhead as we enter the area still remains, though it is now labeled an escape hatch. One other feature remains from the old track layout: the "speed tunnel" near the end of the attraction was left intact, but given a new film so riders could blast the projection of Zurg's spaceship. The Buzz Lightyear attraction uses the same drive mechanism and even the entire track layout unaltered from Take Flight—which had itself been an update of the original attraction here, If You Had Wings. Visitors on the PeopleMover now peer into one room of Buzz Lightyear's Space Ranger Spin, but when Dreamflight occupied this space, they could glance down on both sides of the PeopleMover track and see into separate rooms. These days, unused windows on the left side of the PeopleMover track give testament to the location where visitors used to sneak a peak at the second room. Wooden cutouts of chickens in Buzz Lightyear's Space Ranger Spin also come from the attraction which preceded it. Three chickens just in front of our vehicle in the volcano room of Buzz Lightyear had once occupied the first room of Dreamflight, where whimsical cutout figures celebrated the rural nature of early flight. Another show feature retained from Dreamflight can be seen in the first few scenes, where cloud-shaped bumps alongside the vehicle track frame what visitors can see near the floor. Now painted black, these billowy humps originally represented clouds, in keeping with the aeronautical theme of Dreamflight.

Imagineering Batteries

The cylindrical batteries seen throughout Buzz Lightyear's Space Ranger Spin contain their own inside joke: they are "Made in Glendale," a reference to the home of Walt Disney Imagineering in Glendale, California. Additional versions of these batteries can also be seen in the attraction's queue and exit area.

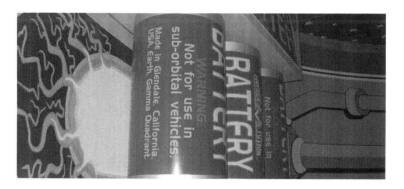

The Tomorrowland Times

One of the static robot statues in Tomorrowland under the PeopleMover displays a remnant from a former time in Tomorrowland. While the Galaxy Gazette seems to be the current newspaper being "sold" by this robot, the former newspaper was called the Tomorrowland Times (which discussed the transportation technology of X-S Tech as seen in Alien Encounter). A hint of the Tomorrowland Times can still be glimpsed through the window of the robot's chest, in a detail that was never updated when Stitch took over Alien Encounter.

Carousel of Progress Sponsor

Walt Disney's Carousel of Progress displays many hints of its original sponsor even long after its sponsorship ended. Conceived for the 1964 World's Fair in New York, the original show (then called Progressland) was sponsored by General Electric, and was designed to show how the company and its household appliances had made life easier over the century. While the narration was adjusted and no longer invoked General Electric by name, the appliances themselves are still present, many are labeled with the GE brand, and some are even animated and still form a central part of the show's theme of progress over the decades. Two of the most prominent are a vacuum cleaner in the 1920s and a refrigerator in the 1940s.

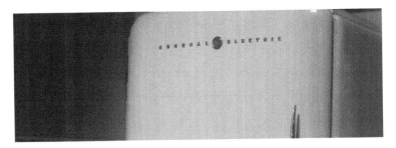

Imagineer Herb Ryman

Longtime Disney artist Herb Ryman, who created many conceptual paintings of Disney theme parks and their attractions, is honored in the second scene of Carousel of Progress (the 1920s). His tribute comes in the form of a billboard in the cityscape seen through the window, which proclaims "Herb Ryman – Attorney at Law." Ryman was the artist who helped Walt create a critical early painting of Disneyland to sell the idea of the park when he needed funding.

Imagineer Marty Sklar

A note stuck to a corkboard in the final scene of Carousel of Progress makes an inside joke about the management of Walt Disney Imagineering. This last scene features a modern household, and far off to the right sits a board where notes and reminders are posted. One prominent note reads "Marty called – wants changes." This might sound like a reference to a document someone is working on, but is an inside joke to the Imagineers. "Marty" refers to Marty Sklar, who for decades was the head of WDI, and a person one could well imagine calling to ask for changes to rides!

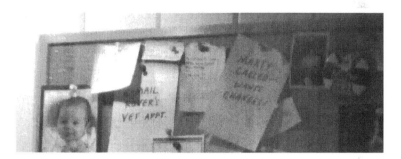

Space Mountain History

The list of "Active Earth Stations" in the first room of Space Mountain's queue includes references to all versions of Space Mountain from around the globe. Sometimes the locations are listed more obviously (Tokyo and Paris), while Anaheim is referenced by its opening date of 1977 and Hong Kong's makes an oblique reference to "E-TKT" or E-Tickets.

Hyperion Studios

A lighted mural in the queue of Space Mountain includes a reference to one of the earliest locations for the Walt Disney Studios. The second mural mentions the term "Hyperion," which is significant in the history of the Disney company. Before the animation studio moved to its present home in Burbank (after the 1937 success of *Snow White and the Seven Dwarfs*), it was located in Hollywood on 2719 Hyperion Avenue.

Space Mountain Opening Date

Space Mountain's opening date of 1975 is commemorated on the attraction's logo. It was built in the 1970s as the world's first enclosed roller-coaster to operate in the dark, preceding even its cousin in Anaheim.

Imagineer John Hench

A longtime artist at the Walt Disney Studios and one of the key Imagineers to build Disneyland and Walt Disney World, John Hench was chosen by Walt to create the first visions of Space Mountain back in the 1960s. The front pod of the spaceship over our heads on the lifthill is labeled H-NCH, a clear reference to John Hench. The year 1975 is referenced alongside Hench's name.

Space Mountain Sponsor

A mechanical dog was crafted as a subtle reference to the attraction's original sponsor, RCA. The mascot for RCA was Nipper, who was famous for his trademark cocked head and floppy ears. When FedEx took over as sponsor of the ride in the 1990s, they created the dioramas still visible today at the exit to the ride and included a mechanical dog crafted for the original sponsor. These dioramas were originally meant to represent far-flung corners of the galaxy, places to which FedEx would ship packages. The control center at the start of the moving sidewalk was originally labeled as a shipping center. FedEx ceased its sponsorship in 2004, and the scenes were later re-themed to vacation destinations rather than created anew.

Mesa Verde

Stickers on "luggage" in the post-show to Space Mountain pay homage to previous attractions that celebrated the future. Stickers include Mesa Verde, the fictional "future city" that was one of the possible endings on Epcot's former ride Horizons, as well as Space Station X-1, which had been an early exhibit in Anaheim's Tomorrowland in 1955.

Sonny Eclipse

Sonny Eclipse, the robotic performer in Cosmic Ray's Starlight Café, is physically a duplicate of Officer Zzyxx, an alien in Tokyo Disneyland that greets visitors in a restaurant called the Pan Galactic Pizza Port. Tokyo's Pan Galactic Pizza Port is referenced a second time in Orlando's Tomorrowland, on a sign glimpsed very briefly from the PeopleMover. Following the model of Progress City on the left, a darkened space displays several neon-accented posters that are illuminated by black light. One of the posters announces "hot delivery" of Pan Galactic Pizza "right to your planet."

Indianapolis Speedway

The Tomorrowland Speedway's former sponsor left traces behind when it departed in 2009. Originally named the Grand Prix Raceway, it offered an international car race. It later became the Tomorrowland Indy Speedway, in honor of the Indianapolis 500 race that sponsored the attraction. The popular race car ride lost its sponsor and most of the decorations in 2009, but one prominent element from the Indy sponsorship remained. A row of bricks marking the start line was meant as an homage to the famous "yard of bricks" at the Indianapolis Motor Speedway, where the track surface was long ago entirely covered with 3.2 million bricks, but 3 feet of original bricks remained at the start line. Having a row of symbolically-significant bricks at the start line was a concept brought over to Orlando as well, and the tribute remains today.

Imagineer Randy Pausch

One artificial leaf blade at the Mad Tea Party offers a quote by a noted Imagineer who died young. The fanciful display of an actual tea party amid the shrubs near the attraction has an oversized leaf with an inscription that reads "Be good at something; it makes you valuable…. Have something to bring to the table, because that will make you more welcome. – Randy Pausch." Randy had been an Imagineer for many years, and found fame late in life as a Carnegie Mellon professor who was offered the chance to participate in the "Last Lecture" series of uplifting speeches, which challenged faculty to give a speech as though it was their last lecture ever to deliver to students, as a way of measuring what's really important in life. Shortly before delivering his planned Last Lecture, Randy discovered he was really terminally ill, which caused him to rethink the contents of that now truly Last Lecture. He turned the occasion into a bestselling book, and when he died, he was honored at Walt Disney World with this inspirational quote.

Former Ticket Booth

Until EPCOT Center opened in 1982, most attractions at Walt Disney World required tickets to ride (ranked A through E), and kiosks were used to sell additional tickets. One such ticket booth survives next to the Many Adventures of Winnie and Pooh, and is used to sell film and small souvenirs. A second ticket booth in Tomorrowland is now used to advertise the Disney Vacation Club.

Mr. Toad's Wild Ride

A painting in the Many Adventures of Winnie the Pooh honors the former occupant of this space, Mr. Toad's Wild Ride. That former ride used characters from the Disney movie *The Wind in the Willows*, including Mr. Toad, Moley, Winky, and others. In today's attraction, the left wall of Owl's house features paintings, one of which shows Mr. Toad handing a piece of paper marked "DEED" over to Owl, implying a transfer of this property from Toad to Winnie the Pooh and his pals. A second painting on the opposite side of the room has "fallen" onto the floor showing Moley, another character from Mr. Toad's Wild Ride, standing with Winnie the Pooh. A third painting, back on the left side of the vehicle in the same room, shows Owl smiling through a handlebar moustache in a tribute to Winky, yet another character from the Toad movie and attraction. To top it off, in this picture Owl is wearing a skimmer straw hat, just like Toad was at the end of his movie.

20,000 Leagues Under the Sea

The tree and its playhouse outside the Many Adventures of Winnie the Pooh pay tribute to the ride which once dominated Fantasyland. Visitors who step inside the room carved out of the base of Pooh's tree will notice a sleek, faded green shape above the doorway, visible only from the inside. This is meant to represent a submarine, for the area was once home to a fleet of half-submerged subs that traveled through a lagoon in an attraction called 20,000 Leagues Under the Sea, loosely based on Disney's 1954 movie of the same name. This tree was built for Pooh's Playful Spot, a temporary playground built on the former location of 20,000 Leagues Under the Sea. When Fantasyland underwent renovations in 2010, the tree moved across the sidewalk to its present location.

Opening Year in Roman Numerals

A sign above the Friar's Nook announces it was established in
MLXXI, or 1071. This matches the medieval setting but still makes
an oblique reference to October, 1971, when the Magic Kingdom
first opened. At various times in its history, this location was called
Lancer's Inn, Gurgi's Munchies & Crunchies, Lumiere's Kitchen and
Village Fry Shoppe.

Disney Family Crest

A crest on the back side of Cinderella Castle displays the Disney
family seal of three lions. This same crest adorns Sleeping Beauty
Castle in Anaheim's Disneyland.

Cinderella Castle Creators

The tile mural of Cinderella fitting her slipper includes tributes to Herb Ryman (the footman) and John Hench (the duke), who helped decide the design and theming of Cinderella Castle.

Coats of Arms

Coats of arms in Cinderella's Royal Table, the restaurant inside
Cinderella Castle, honor people important to the Disney
organization. Coats of arms scattered throughout the interior of the
castle, especially the waiting area and the main dining room of the
restaurant, refer to the family names of many individuals who
helped design and make the Disney theme parks a reality. Some of
these symbols are also visible on the stained glass windows and can
be seen from the outside of the castle, in the courtyard that is home
to the carrousel.

Disney Family Apartment

A large space was set aside in the upper areas of Cinderella Castle when it was first built to serve as an apartment for the Disney family, but it was never fully built or decorated until the 2007 promotion "Year of a Million Dreams." Finally outfitted with furniture and lavish trappings, the "Dream Suite" apartment remains off-limits for normal public viewing. Visitors on the outside can catch a glimpse, though, by looking at the castle from the back side and spying three stained-glass windows 2/3rds of the way up the castle, off to one side.

Sword in the Stone Ceremony

A sword stuck in an anvil in the Fantasyland courtyard was once part of a brief live show involving visitors. Until 2006, several times per day characters from the Disney movie *The Sword in the Stone* would appear and encourage children to try to yank the sword from the anvil. A Cast Member observing from afar would trigger the lock to finally allow the sword to budge, though not fully come free, and a new ruler was crowned.

Miss Liberty

Carved figures atop Prince Charming Regal Carrousel are remnants of this ride's first incarnation. When it was first built in 1917 for the Detroit Palace Garden Park, it was named Miss Liberty and painted patriotic colors. It was purchased in 1967 in Maplewood, New Jersey, and fully reconditioned and repainted for inclusion in the Magic Kingdom.

Mickey Mouse Revue

Mickey Mouse's role as conductor in Mickey's Philharmagic harkens back to a previous attraction at this very location. Before Mickey's Philharmagic opened in 2003, this space was occupied by a live-action puppet show called Legend of the Lion King. Before that, it was the Fantasyland Theater, which showed a 3-D movie called Magic Journeys. Until 1980, this space was home to the Mickey Mouse Revue, a musical show performed by minimalist animatronics of Disney characters, singing songs led by none other than bandleader Mickey Mouse. Other reminders include the posters in the queue for Mickey's Philharmagic, which includes the Three Little Pigs and the Three Caballeros, two acts which had had roles in the Mickey Mouse Revue. This show was moved in its entirety to Tokyo Disneyland, where it played until 2009 . The figures of the seven dwarves were duplicated for the 1994 refurbishment of Snow White's Scary Adventures. Surprisingly, this was not the only instance of recycling the figures from this show. The Alice character, the Mad Hatter, the March Hare, and some flower heads were also removed and taken to Disneyland in 1984, for the major refurbishment of Fantasyland on the West Coast.

Disney Fire Chief Ray Colburn

A wooden barrel at the exit to Peter Pan's Flight is labeled "Fire Chief W. Ray Colburn, Lost Boys Fire Brigade." In reality, Colburn is the longtime chief of the real fire department in Walt Disney World, the semi-governmental agency Reedy Creek Improvement District. A duplicate barrel with this same homage can be found near the exit to Big Thunder Mountain Railroad.

Imagineer Joyce Carlson

One doll in "it's a small world" pays tribute to an artist partly responsible for the ride's look and feel. Joyce Carlson, an Imagineer who assisted in creating the original ride when it premiered at the 1964 World's Fair and later Disneyland, is represented as a doll underneath the Eiffel Tower early in the attraction. Joyce was later placed in charge of installing and maintaining the other versions of the ride around the globe, including the Orlando one. Like Joyce herself, her doll sports big black glasses. The tradition of using a doll to honor the architects of this attraction began at Disneyland, where a doll meant to represent Mary Blair, the primary designer on "it's a small world" and an artist whose distinctive look also graces the murals near the Monorail stop at the Contemporary Resort, can be seen halfway up the Eiffel Tower in California's version of the ride. This doll sports the same yellow coat and black pants which were Mary's trademarks. Even beyond this attraction, there is a long tradition of homages to Disney artists in the finished rides.

Imagineer Leota Thomas

The bronze decorations atop the spires of "it's a small world" are exact copies of one Imagineer's jewelry. Leota Thomas (born Leota Toombs) is well-known to park enthusiasts as Madame Leota in the Haunted Mansion. Her performance as the séance madam was originally intended to be a demonstration only, but designers realized a professional actress would not be able to improve on her performance. She was also known internally at Walt Disney Imagineering for her unique jewelry and earrings. When the Disneyland version of "it's a small world" was being prepared, the sometimes fantastical earrings, pendants, and charms of its chief designer provided a sudden inspiration for the tops of the spires visible on the outdoor façade for the Anaheim attraction. The designs of her jewelry were simply copied and produced on a much larger scale for the attraction's façade. In the Orlando version of the attraction, these bronze toppings look especially like the stud earrings that inspired them, possibly because visitors exit the ride by walking through the spires and thus approach the decorations much more closely than in Anaheim.

Fantasyland Skyway Station

The Skyway station still stands in Fantasyland just past Peter Pan's Flight. It was themed as a Swiss chalet in homage to the origins of the Skyway technology, which Walt had run across in Switzerland. After the ride's closure, the queue area was converted to stroller parking. Near the station in today's Fantasyland, one patch of roughly circular ground with a different texture from the rest of the walkway gives testament to an area that once held a support pylon for the ride, and was filled in after the pylon was removed.

Haunted Mansion FASTPASS

Marked electrical outlets in the cement floor outside the Haunted Mansion were once used for FASTPASS machines. The machines were discontinued in 2006 because the Haunted Mansion had such an impressive capacity even with only a Standby line, and when the machines were taken away, the power supply lines remained behind.

Imagineer Tombstones

Tombstones alongside the queue for the Haunted Mansion honor the Imagineers who helped build the ride. The designers given a tribute here include Xavier Atencio—who wrote the lyrics and script for the show; Marc Davis—who was one of the main creative forces; Yale Gracey—who created many of the illusions; Wathel Rogers—who crafted many of the mechanical effects; Claude Coates—who designed the track layout; Cliff Huet—who was an interior designer; Gordon Williams—who worked with the Audio-Animatronics; Leota Toombs—who performed as the séance madam; Bob Sewell and Dave Burkhart—who crafted many of the models; and Chuck Myall, Fred Joerger, and Bill Martin—who were art directors on the attraction. The Leota tombstone just outside the entrance to the Mansion was the brainchild of Jason Surrell, an Imagineer so enamored with the Haunted Mansion that he wrote a book about the attraction, its history, and its transformation into a live-action motion picture. Every few seconds, the eyes of the face on this tombstone flutter open, look about, then close again.

Mr. Toad's Tombstone

Just outside the exit to the Haunted Mansion, a graveyard ostensibly for pets includes statues and grave markers for dogs, cats, and birds. Back in the far left corner, a humble statue of Mr. Toad himself provides a whimsical tribute to this character, who is "dead" because his ride can no longer be found at the Magic Kingdom after it was replaced by a dark ride dedicated to Winnie the Pooh.

Haunted Mansion's Original Narrator

Almost every time Guests hear the voice of the Ghost Host, the raven is nearby. In the original plans for the attraction, the bird was supposed to be the Ghost Host, the narrator of the ride. The raven, long associated with death in several cultures, is present in the conservatory on the moving coffin, in the séance room on the chair, in the Ballroom along the rear wall, right outside the attic, and at the end of the graveyard, just as visitors enter the crypt.

Mr. Lincoln in the Haunted Mansion

One of the Mansion's creepiest optical effects, the busts in the library that appear to turn their heads in sync as the "Doom Buggies" pass by them, actually owes its existence to Great Moments with Mr. Lincoln, a Disneyland-only forerunner to the Hall of Presidents. Designers happened to pass by a negative mold of the Lincoln head—an inverted cast from which the actual head would be made—when they realized that its inverted nature always resulted in the unnerving effect.

Museum of the Weird

Disembodied arms holding torches at the exit to Haunted Mansion are but one of many remnants of a "Museum of the Weird" concept. There was a Walt-era idea to create a museum in Disneyland's New Orleans Square dedicated to strange, supernatural, and occult items, such as might be found in a gypsy's wagon. These concepts were incorporated into the Haunted Mansion in the form of furniture and trappings of the house that seem to be alive but disembodied or unnatural. Besides the arms holding torches, other examples include the clock striking 13 (watch for a face with fangs, and the clock's pendulum as a tail) or the gypsy-like cart outside Orlando's Haunted Mansion selling merchandise. These designs were all the work of one Imagineer named Rolly Crump.

Carousel of Progress Grandmother

The ghostly woman in a rocking chair at the Ballroom scene of the Haunted Mansion is a duplicate figure from another attraction. The Audio-Animatronics figure is a duplicate of the grandmother in Carousel of Progress. The first versions of both of these rides were conceived and built in the 1960s, so it made sense to re-use the molds of existing Audio-Animatronics whenever possible.

Voice Actor Thurl Ravenscroft

One of the iconic singing busts in the graveyard scene of the Haunted Mansion shows a video projection of prolific voice actor Thurl Ravenscroft, who lent his deep voice to popular cultural touchstones like Tony the Tiger and *How the Grinch Stole Christmas*. For the Disney parks, Thurl was the voice of parrot Fritz in the Tiki Room, Buff in the Country Bear Jamboree, frogs in Splash Mountain, several pirates in Pirates of the Caribbean, and the lead singer in the song Grim Grinning Ghosts. Thurl's projection is on the broken statue which is sometimes mistaken for Walt Disney's face.

Indoor Tombstones

The tombstones in the finale sequence of the Haunted Mansion, which takes place in the graveyard, also pay tribute to Imagineers on the attraction. In some cases, though, the names of the Imagineers are scrambled. One tombstone near the track pays homage to Judi

Gray, Fred Joerger, and Harriet Burns, all model-builders, but their names are listed with the letters in randomized order.

Headless Horseman

The Haunted Mansion is modeled after houses where the Headless Horseman story was set. Houses built in the 18th century in the picturesque Hudson River Valley, now a National Heritage area and home to well-preserved dwellings from several different epochs in American history, provided the thematic inspiration for the general look of the Haunted Mansion. The Hudson River Valley is also the setting for the legend of Sleepy Hollow and the Headless Horseman—a perfect thematic fit for the Haunted Mansion. At the other end of Liberty Square, an eatery named "Sleepy Hollow Refreshments" provides a thematic bookend for the land. This building was inspired by the real Hudson River Valley house of the Sleepy Hollow author, Washington Irving. Across the way from Sleepy Hollow Refreshments, a sign states that the proprietor of the music lessons shop is none other than Ichabod Crane, who did a fair amount of singing in the original story. A Headless Horseman can even sometimes be seen at the Magic Kingdom. During Mickey's Not So Scary Halloween Party, a Headless Horseman thunders down the parade route before the party's parade.

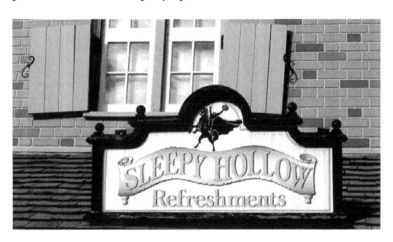

Presidential Voices

Actors provided the voices for George Washington and Abraham Lincoln in the early years of the Hall of Presidents. Bill Clinton was the first sitting president to lend his voice to a speech, and George W. Bush and Barack Obama continued the tradition. The show was renovated and modernized in several ways for its reopening after Obama's inauguration.

Lincoln-Douglas Debates

Two paintings hanging in the exit lobby of the Hall of Presidents were used in the original version of the show. When a refurbishment was undertaken in 2008, several scenes were cut from the show's movie while others were added. One of the paintings showing Lincoln debating with Douglas was kept for the new show, but the other was not. However, it remained hanging in the post-show corridor.

Walt Disney's Grandfather

A sign outside Ye Olde Christmas Shoppe honors Walt Disney's grandfather. This sign facing the Liberty Bell replica says "Kepple" with the date 1779, in honor of Kepple Disney. This shop is themed to represent three different stores combined over time. Differences in furniture colors and styles, as well as highly varied wallpaper styles, point to the implied history of the merchandise location as one that conglomerated out of three different shops. Trinkets atop shelves in each area attest to the previous residents in each shop: a musician, a woodcarver, and a German family identified as Kepple. In fact, the backstory for the shop is what actually happened. The presence of three separate areas in the Christmas Shoppe can be traced to the fact that originally, there were three distinct stores here! The Christmas Shoppe replaced Mlle. Lafayette's Parfumerie, the Silversmith, and Old World Antiques.

Steamboat Original Names

The Liberty Square Riverboat was originally named the Richard F. Irvine. At first there were two steamboats plying the waters of the Rivers of America: the Admiral Joe Fowler and the Richard F. Irvine, named after two company executives who had done much to help build Walt Disney World. A dry-dock accident permanently crippled the Fowler when it was misaligned during the draining of the water, and after it was sidelined, the Irvine was renamed to the Liberty Belle, though park maps refer to it as the Liberty Square Riverboat. To honor the Irvine, one of its life preservers was kept with the original name for several years. To continue the tradition of honoring these men who did so much to help the Disney company, two of the ferries used to transport guests from the Ticket and Transportation Center to the theme park, named Magic Kingdom-1 and Magic Kingdom-2, were renamed to the Admiral Joe Fowler and Richard F. Irvine. A third ferry is named the General Joe Potter, another figure responsible for building Walt Disney World.

Admiral Joe Fowler

Just as the original Irvine was honored with an unaltered life preserver, the original Fowler was likewise kept alive, in the form of its whistle, which was relocated to the fourth locomotive on the Walt Disney World Railroad, the Roy O. Disney.

Opening Year of the Magic Kingdom

A crate along the Rivers of America (roughly near the Frontierland Shootin' Gallery, and facing the water) marks yet another celebration of the year the Magic Kingdom opened, in 1971.

Canoe Dock

The unused dock near the exit to Big Thunder Mountain Railroad was once used for a canoe attraction. The Davy Crockett Explorer Canoes were guest-powered free floating canoes on the river. They operated until 1994.

Wilson's Cave Inn

Visible only from the steamboat, a show scene of a keelboat in a cave known as Wilson's Cave Inn (a pun on "cave in") honors an actual location in the Midwest. Cave-In-Rock in Illinois, along the banks of the Ohio River, was similarly shaped and had been a hideout and even a tavern—Wilson's Liquor Vault—in the late 1700s. These real river pirates, in turn, inspired a Disney-made Davy Crockett movie in the 1950s that spurred interest in the frontier and made Disneyland a must-visit destination. Keel boats from the Crockett movies were used at Disneyland, and the idea was brought over to the Magic Kingdom years later.

Mike Fink Keelboats

Keelboats were small flat-bottomed boats used for navigating shallow waters, and had been made fashionable by Disney's Davy Crockett movies. The Mike Fink Keel Boats at the Magic Kingdom were located next to the Haunted Mansion. A nearby shop took on relevant names over the years, such as Keelboat Shop, Keelboat Hat Shop, and Ichabod's Landing, but it closed in 1996. The keelboats moved from here in 1998 to another location near Big Thunder Mountain, and eventually closed completely in 2001. Today, the former dock can still be seen along the river near the Haunted Mansion, though it is presently unused.

Michael Jackson's Thriller Video

A key visual element of the video to Michael Jackson's *Thriller* (1982)—a hand shooting out of the earth by a tombstone—owes its existence to the shooting gallery at Walt Disney World. Michael admitted to Disney designers that their tombstone in Disneyland and Walt Disney World had inspired the video for him.

Harper's Mill

Harper's Mill, a structure on Tom Sawyer Island named for Imagineer and Studio artist Harper Goff, is home to a unique Disney film reference in the form of a bluebird nest. This is an homage to the Disney cartoon *The Old Mill* (1937), primarily famous today for its introduction of the multiplane camera.

Walt's Childhood Fort

Fort Langhorn on Tom Sawyer Island is a creative descendant of Walt's childhood fort. While watching Walt dictate a revised placement for Fort Wilderness at Disneyland's Tom Sawyer Island, his brother Roy realized that Walt was re-creating a makeshift fort they had often built on a sand spit out on a river as children. Orlando's version, Fort Langhorn, was named after the author Mark Twain, whose real name was Samuel Langhorn Clemens. This fort, once called simply Fort Sam Clemens, can be seen as another recreation of Walt's childhood fort.

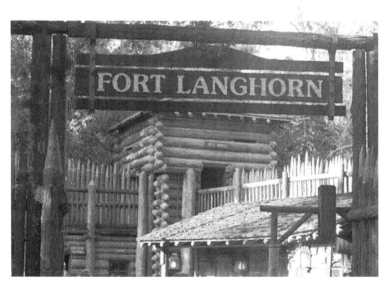

Fort Langhorn Cantina

A former counter-service location inside the fort on Tom Sawyer Island has been closed for some years, but the shuttered order windows are still plainly visible, and making their presence even more explicit, there are jars labeled "Provisions" on shelves just above these windows. The fort was originally named Fort Sam Clemens (Mark Twain's real name), but to avoid confusion with narration aboard watercraft it was renamed to Langhorn, which was Clemens's middle name.

Aunt Polly's

Once a quick-service location serving ice cream and smaller snacks on Tom Sawyer Island, Aunt Polly's closed in 2006. It faced the riverboat dock, and its structure, as well as a sign proclaiming Aunt Polly's, can still be seen.

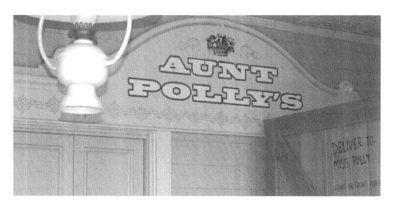

Disneyland TV Series

The sign for the Frontier Trading Post claims it is run by "Texas John Slaughter"; this is a reference to a similarly-named series on the *Disneyland* TV show from 1958-1961.

Marc Davis Wagon

A tribute to Imagineer Marc Davis, added in 2010, can be found on a crate near the Country Bear Jamboree labeled "Davis Tobacco." Davis had been partly responsible for the Country Bear Jamboree show, so the location of this tribute is fitting.

Sponsor Pepsi

Henry, the host bear in the Country Bear Jamboree, early in the show invokes the phrase "we've got a lot to give." This line is an audio remnant of the show's first sponsor, Pepsi, who used the same tagline at the time in the early 1970s.

Imagineer Al Bertino

The bear "Big Al" in the Country Bear Jamboree is a loving caricature of one of the show's co-creators, Al Bertino. Together with Marc Davis, Bertino had originally designed this show for use at the planned Mineral Springs Ski Resort in California, though ultimately Walt Disney opted not to develop this property since the infrastructure and roads were not adequate to lure sufficient visitors. This show has had several variations, including the Country Bear Vacation Hoedown (1986-2001) and the Country Bear Christmas Special (1984-2006).

Mine Train Through Nature's Wonderland

The staging of animal encounters on Big Thunder Mountain Railroad pays tribute to the ride which was its creative ancestor. When Big Thunder Mountain Railroad first premiered at Disneyland it replaced Mine Train Through Nature's Wonderland, a slow-moving train ride through desert scenes and tableaus of robotic animals interacting with their surroundings in various ways. Some of those interactions are recreated at the Magic Kingdom's version of Big Thunder Mountain Railroad. Examples include the bobcat taking refuge from three attacking boars atop a cactus, and a face-off between a roadrunner and a snake, both of which take place in the town of Tumbleweed. The dramatic splashdown at the finale into a dinosaur skeleton was reproduced from Anaheim, where the placing of a skeleton was itself a tribute to a dinosaur skeleton seen during Mine Train Through Nature's Wonderland.

Splash Mountain Gopher

One gopher deep inside Splash Mountain roots for a real-life sports team. A series of gophers pop out of gopher holes in the ground in the area just prior to the big lift hill and before the big drop. The final gopher drops down from a hole in the ceiling and loudly exclaims "FSU!" This startlingly clear reference to Florida State University comes from the Imagineer responsible for the gophers, who had graduated from FSU and remained a fan of its football team. Disneyland's Splash Mountain was built to utilize a motley collection of animals from the musical show America Sings, a

Tomorrowland attraction that replaced Carousel of Progress in Disneyland and celebrated the history of music in America. Numerous weasels in that show were deployed at Splash Mountain popping up out of gopher holes, implying the same robotic performers were now to be considered gophers! When the Orlando version was built, gophers were newly created. They also duplicated many of the other animals from America Sings rather than create new ones from scratch.

French Fry Cart
A stagecoach wheel just to the right of the Golden Oak Outpost is a remnant and inside joke from the former French Fry cart that preceded the Golden Oak Outpost on this spot. The Golden Oak Outpost was built as a new structure in 2009, but prior to that this area had been home to a smaller cart themed to look like a stagecoach that had broken down and lost one wheel, which was off to the side. The broken wheel was retained as a tribute when the new facility was constructed.

Imagineer Marc Davis

One of the major creative forces behind Pirates of the Caribbean, animator and Imagineer Marc Davis is honored at the conclusion of the ride with his family's personal coat-of-arms, displayed high on the exterior wall of the "treasure room" at the very end of the ride.

Mighty Ducks of Anaheim

The birds in the preshow of the Tiki Room Under New Management are portrayed as bickering talent agents for avian performers. One of them makes reference to being on the cusp of signing the Mighty Ducks hockey team, a remnant from the days when the Walt Disney Company created and held ownership of the team, which took its name, not surprisingly, from an eponymous Disney movie.

Florida Citrus Growers

Vestiges of the original sponsor remain at the Sunshine Tree Terrace. In its early years, the Tiki Room, then known as the

Tropical Serenade, was sponsored by the Florida Citrus Growers. This local association wanted to promulgate the vision of the state as sunny, warm, and welcoming, and it sought to market Florida oranges as superior to all others. It was a natural fit that the association also sponsor the nearby Sunshine Tree Terrace, which served citrus drinks. The association's mascot, the Orange Bird, even maintained a presence at the Magic Kingdom, appearing as both a walkaround character and a figurine in the artificial tree that "sprouted" out of the counter-service location and gave it its name. Although the artificial tree is long gone and the Sunshine Tree Terrace now sports a misleading name, there are reminders of the association's presence in the décor. Just under the thatched roof is a pattern repeated around the entire structure: a round, orange-colored object, clearly a reference to the citrus fruit which the association wanted to ingrain in people's minds. These painted oranges survived the transition from a sponsor-driven location to a less specific theme.

Elephant Tales

Signs in the shops of Adventureland reference a bygone store. Located in the buildings behind the open-air Agrabah Bazaar, Elephant Tales once housed an upscale clothing store when it opened in 1988. Today, signs with the words "Elephant Tales" can still be seen along a back wall of the Bazaar.

Stitch Kingdom

An infrequent sound byte heard in the background music in the bathrooms of the Magic Kingdom is a remnant from an old advertising campaign. When Stitch's Great Escape was new in 2004, the park was marketed as though Stitch was loose in the park and wreaking havoc everywhere. Artwork showed an animated Stitch spray-painting "Stitch" over the word "Magic" as if to rename the place Stitch Kingdom, and audio spiels in the monorail reflected the same mythos. As part of the effort, Stitch's distinctive cackle was added to the music loops playing in the bathrooms around the park, though the sound is not explained and does not repeat often. It can still be heard in those music loops, especially in the Adventureland and Tomorrowland bathrooms.

Imagineer Morgan Evans

One address on the Jungle Cruise FASTPASS machines refers to Morgan Evans, the landscaper who assembled the lush horticulture of both Disneyland and the Magic Kingdom. The FASTPASS machine is themed like an oversized shipping crate, so it naturally needs an address label. This label states that Morgan Evans can be found at 1313 Harbor Blvd, which is Disneyland's street address

(Disneyland's zip code is 92803, but 71755 refers to Disneyland's opening date of July 17, 1955). A nearby planter in the walkway also references Evans.

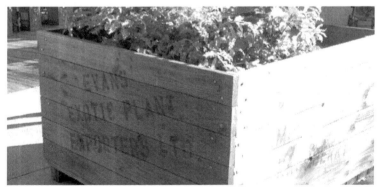

Adventurer's Club

Several tags for artifacts in the first part of the Jungle Cruise queue make reference to the Adventurer's Club at Pleasure Island. The live-skit and improv comedy show at the Adventurer's Club made for a unique form of interactive entertainment, but it closed in 2008. It is no coincidence that Disney's Animal Kingdom shares traits and sensibilities with the Adventurer's Club. One of designer Joe Rohde's first projects for Disney was the Adventurer's Club, which presaged his later work at Disney's Animal Kingdom on a number of levels: a mishmash of world cultures, a clutter of artifacts, and a counter-culture vibe in the entire operation. Joe was assisted in designing the Adventurer's Club by magician Doug Henning, who crafted the illusions in the show. While 5189 Hill St. isn't the street address of the former comedy club in Pleasure Island, it still has a connection: May 1, 1989 was the opening date of the club, otherwise written as 5/1/89.

Imagineer Wathel Rogers

A sign just inside the entrance to the Jungle Cruise queue pays homage to the Imagineer who gave life to many robotic creations at the Disney parks. Listed on the sign as an animal handler, Wathel Rogers was actually a sculptor who helped create Project Little Man, which led to the development of Audio-Animatronics. He also had a hand in most Audio-Animatronics that followed.

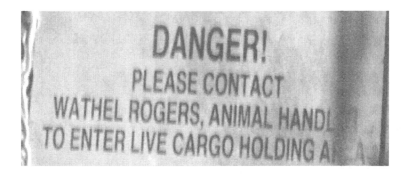

Imagineer Winston Hibler

One barrel in the queue for the Jungle Cruise is addressed to Dr. Winston Hibler, Special Arachnid Unit, Jungle Exploration Company, Outpost #71755. Winston Hibler was the narrator on all the True-Life Adventure films of the 1950s, which largely formed the basis for the Adventureland concept. He was also the unheralded speechwriter for Walt Disney's dedication of Disneyland which opened on July 17, 1955. Hence, the mention of Outpost #71755 acknowledges Hibler's role in Disneyland's grand opening.

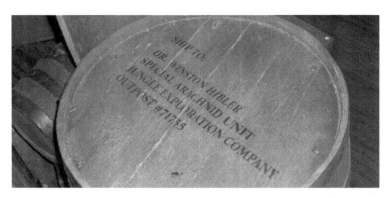

Imagineer Harper Goff

Near the end of the queue at the Jungle Cruise, next to a red oil
drum, rests a crate labeled "Goff's Brand" of crocodile resistant pants,
which pays homage to the main designer of Disneyland's Main
Street, Harper Goff. The fictional brand has its ostensible base at
"1911 Main Street, Fort Collins, Colorado," a tribute not only to
Goff's role in creating Main Street, but also to his hometown of Fort
Collins that provided the inspiration for both Disneyland's bank and
city hall. Even the supposed street address has significance; 1911 was
the year of Goff's birth (he died in 1993).

July 17

An ammo crate in the Jungle Cruise, at the scene where gorillas have overturned a jeep, makes reference to Disneyland's opening in 1955 on July 17. The crate is labeled "Ammo 717"—variations of 7/17 are common throughout the Disney parks to pay homage to the original Disney theme park.

Spartacus

The actor who fought against Kirk Douglas in Spartacus lives on at Disneyland and Walt Disney World in the form of the natives seen in the Jungle Cruise. When building the first Jungle Cruise, Imagineer Harper Goff called on Woody Strode, the actor from Spartacus, to create a mold of his body from which they could make the needed figures of the natives.

Swiss Family Robinson Director and Actors

Crates at the exit to the Jungle Cruise—near the Swiss Family
Treehouse—honor people associated with the book and movie.
Kenneth Annakin, the director of the *Swiss Family Robinson* movie,
is honored with a crate at the Jungle Cruise exit. The address on this
crate makes mention of New Guinea, which was to be the original
destination of the Robinsons before they were marooned. A crate
just below it is addressed to Johann David Wyss, who authored the
original novel, and it is being sent to McGuire Blvd, the joke being
that Dorothy McGuire was the actress who played the mother in the
movie. There is also a reference to John Mills, the actor who played
Father Robinson. The reference to John Mills includes an address on
"Bora Danno," a convoluted tribute to James MacArthur, the actor
who played son Fritz Robinson. To understand the tribute, one must
first know that MacArthur later portrayed Detective Danny
Williams in "Hawaii Five-0," the character whose nickname was
"Danno."

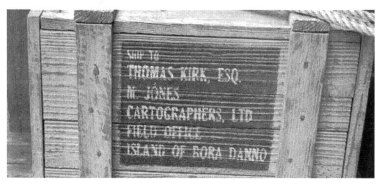

Shrunken Ned

The remote-controlled boats near the Jungle Cruise are labeled as belonging to Shrunken Ned, who is not otherwise explained in this park. This is an homage to a Shrunken Ned at Disneyland, who is a coin-operated fortune teller.

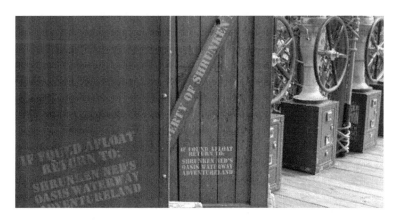

Latin Names for Plants and Trees

Throughout the Magic Kingdom, tiny brass plaques announce the scientific Latin names of several varieties of trees, shrubs, and plants. This is a tradition that began in Anaheim's Disneyland and was continued here when the East Coast Magic Kingdom opened up. Originally, it was born out of necessity. As the opening day of Disneyland approached in 1955 and not enough rides and shows were operating, Walt Disney ordered that many of the trees and plants be identified by their Latin names and described in a few sentences, to provide at least an educational exhibit that might make up for the relative lack of attractions on opening day.

Disneyland's Birthday on the Treehouse

There are no accidental occurrences of "July 17" at Disney parks, and the sign at the Swiss Family Robinson pays yet more tribute to the opening of Disneyland in 1955.

Bob Hope

Bwana Bob's was named after comedian Bob Hope, a central figure in Disney theme park history. This store in Adventureland, originally called the "Adventureland Kiosk," was renamed Bwana Bob's in 1985 to honor Bob Hope, who was a personal friend of Walt Disney and who had taken part in Walt Disney World's official opening years before. Bob had starred in a 1963 film named *Call Me Bwana*, which inspired the first half of the store's name. Bob was present at the opening ceremonies for several Disney parks, including Disneyland, the Magic Kingdom, and Disney's Hollywood Studios (then Disney-MGM Studios), where he officially opened the park by cutting the ceremonial opening day ribbon. Bob was heavily involved in one version of the story of Soviet Premier Nikita Khrushchev's desired visit to Disneyland. At a political event Bob paid Disneyland a compliment in conversation with the premier's wife, prompting the premier to try to arrange a visit. When the U.S. Secret Service nixed the idea, saying they couldn't guarantee his safety, Khrushchev's visible anger was televised around the world and became an international incident. Never one to pass up an opportunity—even one he had had an inadvertent hand in creating—Bob Hope turned it into a joke during a performance in

Alaska, which he called "halfway between Khrushchev and Disneyland."

Epcot

Presidents on Spaceship Earth

Numerous Audio-Animatronics figures in Spaceship Earth are duplicates of U.S. Presidents used elsewhere at Walt Disney World. In Spaceship Earth, the characters are either unknowns or unfamiliar faces, and faces "borrowed" from historical figures were perfectly acceptable. Because Spaceship Earth called for so many Audio-Animatronics figures, it was deemed simpler to make use of the molds in place for the numerous figures created for the Magic Kingdom's Hall of Presidents. Teddy Roosevelt is used twice—once as an Egyptian priest and again a Roman senator—but most cameos are single: Franklin Pierce and John Tyler are Islamic scholars, James Buchanan portrays Gutenberg, Dwight Eisenhower plays the lute, and Ulysses S. Grant appears as a sculptor. Several figures in Spaceship Earth also come from the American Adventure. Look for Andrew Carnegie at the printing press and Matthew Brady as the telegraph operator, among others.

WDI on Spaceship Earth

The park design arm of the company, Walt Disney Imagineering, is famous for leaving behind subtle nods to itself. On Spaceship Earth, this once took the form of a radio booth microphone bearing the initials WED, as though that were the name of a radio station. But WED (short for Walter Elias Disney) was the name of the park design division that would later be renamed as Walt Disney Imagineering. A 2008 revision to Spaceship Earth altered the microphone's tribute to instead say WDI.

Original Theme of Spaceship Earth

Most of the vignettes in Spaceship Earth revolve around communication, especially written communication. The storyline, originally developed with the aid of science-fiction writer Ray Bradbury, traces a continuing metaphor of writing on walls that eventually graduates into portable, and then digital, communications. An upgrade to the attraction in 2007 morphed the theme somewhat, especially in the sets near the end of the attraction, away from communication and toward technology in general, which was a better match for new sponsor Siemens. A lengthy scene involving communication across the World Wide Web was replaced with a historical look at room-sized computers and then the garage-based birth of the personal computer.

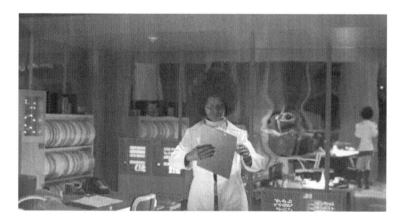

WorldKey Video Restaurant Reservations

Adjacent to Guest Relations, a curved wall with boarded windows is all that remains of a video restaurant reservation system called WorldKey. Patrons would step up to one of the video monitors to discover a live feed of a reservation attendant, who could also see and hear the patrons via a camera mounted nearby, and the reservations were made just by having a conversation. Essentially video conferencing, the system wasn't more efficient than a face to face reservations counter would have been, but it did have an air of futurism. The location next to Guest Relations was the second home for WorldKey, which was originally situated at the exit to Spaceship Earth.

Universe of Energy

One line of the narrator's monologue in Ellen's Energy Adventure
pays tribute to the attraction which preceded it. As our theater
vehicles pull into the last room to hear the Final Jeopardy answers,
the disembodied Jeopardy narrator waxes poetic about energy:
"Energy: you make the world go around!" This line is a direct quote
of the title of a song written by Robert Moline used at the original
Universe of Energy pavilion, which featured a celebrity-free
variation of the same ride, sets, and movie screens. The original
attraction explained the world of energy sources, but without
today's humorous narrative storyline.

Energy Information Center

In one film, Ellen and Bill visit a solar electric plant, where Ellen
discovers she can control the weather by snapping her fingers.
While this footage is new, the overhead shots of the rows of mirrors
at this real facility in the Mojave Desert in California date back to
the film used in the original Energy attraction. This portion of the
ride was named the Energy Information Center, during which a
wide-format film explained the varieties and possibilities of
alternative fuels.

Riding on Sunshine

The roof of the Energy pavilion is covered with 80,000 photovoltaic
cells that generate 75 kilowatts of power, enough power for more
than ten residential homes. In the original Universe of Energy,
visitors were informed that this solar energy was captured to help

power their traveling theater cars, so they had been "riding on sunshine" for the entire show.

Multiplane Animation

The widescreen animation of Earth's formation seen in Ellen's Energy Adventure is a holdover from the original attraction, and historically significant for its use of a multiplane camera to create the illusion of traveling through an animated three dimensional world. Originally invented in the 1930s, the multiplane camera had sat unused at the Disney Studios for over twenty years when it was resurrected for the Energy pavilion. This original multiplane camera later went on display at the One Man's Dream exhibit in Disney's Hollywood Studios.

Horizons

Mission: Space honors its predecessor by displaying the old logo in the gift shop. Housed in a diamond-shaped building where Mission: Space now stands, Horizons offered a ride through sets and movie screens that celebrated futurism, using an "Omnimover" ride system like the one still in use at the Haunted Mansion. The logo for Horizons, a stylized set of straight lines through a central circle, can be seen on the front side of the counter in the gift shop at the attraction's exit.

That same logo from Horizons can also be found in today's Mission:

Space queue at the center of the enormous gravity wheel. This wheel was a giant set piece from the movie *Mission to Mars* that had to be modified to fit into this building. The X-1 model overhead was also a prop from the movie.

Mission to Mars Crash Landing

A video playing in one monitor at the mission control room of Mission: Space's queue honors the attraction's creative ancestor. The illuminated but deserted mission control room seen at the end of the queue is a tribute all by itself to Mission to Mars, the theme park attraction once found at Disneyland and at the Magic Kingdom. This is the original piece of equipment from Mission to Mars! The homage is made much more explicit by a brief movie clip on one of the console monitors that shows an albatross coming in for a "crash landing." This exact video figured prominently as comic relief in the Mission to Mars control room preshow, but at Mission: Space it only shows every once in a while, as it is part of a much longer loop of other videos. Furthering the inside joke, the onetime host of Mission to Mars, Mr. Johnson, is paged every so often in Mission: Space in that very control room.

Mr. Johnson from Mission to Mars

The voiceover at the very last briefing of Mission: Space mentions Mr. Johnson, the former Mission to Mars robotic host: "Attention Mr. Johnson, check the radar." This message is played over the "gantry cam" while visitors are waiting to board, and is usually only heard when there is a significant delay in boarding.

World of Motion

A car in the Test Track queue area honors the attraction which preceded it. The white car elevated on blocks, seen near the start of the queue for Test Track, was used in the previous pavilion to stand on this spot, the World of Motion. That attraction celebrated the evolution of mankind's ability to travel on the ground, and in particular, the role played by the automobile. The sponsor for the transportation pavilion, first as World of Motion and then Test Track, has been General Motors from the beginning. The exit to the attraction has always had a showroom for GM cars and prototypes, though the "Transcenter" theme to the World of Motion's exit area included more diverse offerings, such as the brief animated film "Water Engine" or the vaudeville robot performers "Bird and the Robot."

Test Track Opening Date

Signs in the queue and in the ride itself allude to the attraction's planned opening date. A green highway sign reading "Florida 97" at the end of the queue in Test Track (and seen again at the split between Track-A and Track-B in the middle of the attraction) was meant to refer to the attraction's opening date, but the reference is garbled because the ride opened two years behind schedule. Originally scheduled to open in May 1997, the attraction had all of its show elements (including these tribute signs) installed on time, but its experimental ride mechanisms led to delays and the ride was not ready for the public until March 1999.

A President in Test Track

The driver of the semi-trailer truck that almost hits our car in Test Track is a former President of the United States! A dark alley between the winding S-turns of the hills and the crash test is punctuated by the sudden appearance of a semi-trailer truck, which forces visitors' vehicles to swerve. Because the event is so brief and so sudden, and because the truck shines its headlights directly at the car, few visitors notice who is driving: a cardboard cutout of former president Lyndon Baines Johnson. He is rendered even more unrecognizable with accoutrements such as a flower lei, a hat, and sunglasses.

Thermal Image Photo

On-ride audio on Test Track makes reference to the original location of the on-ride photo available for sale. When riders complete the high-speed loop and are slowed down for re-entry into the building, we hear via speakers "As long as they're heated up, let's grab a thermal image." Visitors then see a multicolored thermal image of their bodies in the car, but this zone originally did double-duty as a place to also snap the on-ride (regular) photo later offered for sale. Because many people's expressions had reverted to a more sedate arrangement by this point in the ride, however, it was later decided to move the on-ride photo snap to the moment just before "impact" with the crash wall, when people are more likely to be screaming.

Kidcot

A metal mesh wall in the shop at Test Track is a remnant of the Kidcot child activity in Future World. The Future World Kidcot activity ceased in 2009, although the World Showcase version continued on. Most of these freestanding walls were removed in the other pavilions, but one remained in Inside Track and another one on the second floor of the Seas pavilion.

The Living Seas

The lifeguard station visible early in the queue for The Seas With Nemo and Friends includes a tribute to the original Living Seas pavilion. The original pavilion cultivated the fiction that visitors were taken deep below the surface to an undersea research facility

named Seabase Alpha. The lifeguard stand prominently displays the number 5A, an oblique reference to the initials for Seabase Alpha (using a numeral instead of a letter). Nearby in the queue, a sign mentions 1401 Coral Coast Hwy, a reference to the address of Walt Disney Imagineering, at 1401 Flower St. in Glendale. Those seeking hidden characters will note the Hidden Nemo and Hidden Squirt in the cut glass at the end of the loading dock. Others seeking yet more references to the former pavilion must wait for the end of the ride. Mr. Ray's overhead voice at the unload dock exclaims "Sea Cab knowledge, that's why we explore!"—a reference to the original "sea cab" vehicles that traversed the fish tank, though without additional theming. In the second floor observation deck of the main aquarium, glance overhead to spot now-dormant monitors, which used to provide information about the types of fish before us, back when the focus of the pavilion was more about education than entertainment. Lastly, the pavilion's original commemoration plaque still hangs on a wall near the exit door.

Imagineer Fulton Burley

A casual reference in the sea cab voiceover at The Seas With Nemo and Friends honors a longtime Disney voice actor. In the voiceover, we hear mention of Commander Fulton, a reference to voice actor Fulton Burley, the voice of Michael in the Tiki Room. He worked a total of 25 years at Disneyland's Golden Horseshoe Revue, alongside Wally Boag (also present in the Tiki Room as José). Fulton Burley enjoys numerous tributes at Walt Disney World. In addition to the reference at the Seas with Nemo and Friends, his name appears at Fulton's General Store in Port Orleans Riverside, and again at Downtown Disney, in the lessee-operated restaurant Fulton's Crab House.

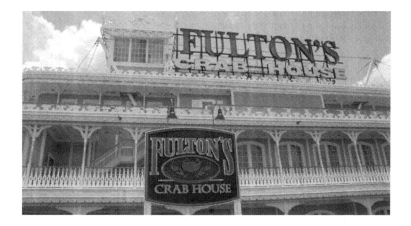

The Living Seas Sea Cabs

The corridor visible along the bottom of the big aquarium of The Seas with Nemo and Friends contains the "EAC" portion of the ride, but also preserves a remnant of the former attraction here. Before it became The Seas with Nemo and Friends, this pavilion was host to a more scientific-oriented celebration and exploration of liquid space, and it boasted a much more modest Omnimover ride past the same picture windows into the big aquarium. Because there was no East Australian Current to watch in the long tube, passengers simply looked to windows on either side, as well as some directly overhead. While those windows cannot be seen from inside the tube now, they can still clearly be seen from the upstairs observation post after exiting the ride. Television monitors in that observation deck are also leftovers from the educational element of the pavilion in its former incarnation.

Turtle Talk With Crush

A wall-sized screen in one corner of the Seas with Nemo and Friends was the former home of Turtle Talk with Crush. When it originally opened, Turtle Talk with Crush was found in the downstairs bay nearest the manatee exhibit, but the lack of a dedicated waiting area made for long lines in the central courtyard of the pavilion. Turtle Talk moved in 2007, three years after its initial opening, to the current location near the ride. When it departed, the main screen once used to display Crush remained behind.

Seabase Alpha

The illusion of the Seabase being on the ocean floor is a carefully cultivated one that dates back to this pavilion's roots as the Living Seas. As Seabase Alpha on the bottom of the ocean, this pavilion was supposedly deep underwater, and large half-domes in the ceiling of the main area attested to this fact. Inside, projected lights created the illusion of sunlight rippling across the surface of the ocean, ostensibly far above us. This effect dates back to the original Seabase Alpha. A similar effect of water rippling can still be seen in the second floor, just above the waiting area for Turtle Talk.

Symbiosis

A plaque outside the Land pavilion refers to symbiosis, the original guiding principle behind the pavilion. All attractions in the original pavilion made reference to the need for a balanced approach to humanity's interaction with nature: they were the Kitchen Kabaret animatronic stage show (balanced nutrition), the Listen to the Land boat ride (balanced approach to farming), and the film actually named *Symbiosis* (balanced relationship with the land). The movie *Circle of Life: An Environmental Fable* (1995) replaced *Symbiosis*, an eighteen-minute video about the complex interrelationship between humans and the earth, although some of the scenes in *Symbiosis* were kept intact for the new movie and can still be seen today. The pavilion's emphasis on the living plants of the planet is obvious, but the pavilion also honors the physical earth and its multifarious composition via the jumbled tile murals just outside the main doors, meant to capture the layers of the planet's crust. The pavilion's overall shape is meant to evoke a volcano, so it makes sense that we would pass through layers of the planet's crust on our way inside. Elements of the philosophy of symbiosis can still be glimpsed in the décor of the Land pavilion, where colorful balloons in the central courtyard, as well as the name of the nearby food court, make reference in their markings to the four seasons, as if implying the need for a harmonious relationship with nature through all the seasons. These balloons were originally decorated to symbolize the basic food groups.

Original Land Pavilion Logo

When EPCOT Center was new, each pavilion of Future World had its own unique stylized symbol. As the pavilions were updated in the 1990s and beyond, these symbols were phased out of active use, and the one at the Land was officially retired in 2005 when the area was refurbished and re-themed for the opening of Soarin'. However, the symbol, a leaf in a globe, remains on the FASTPASS machines at Living with the Land and provides a link to the past.

Epcot's Opening Year

A subtle sign in Living with the Land honors the year Epcot first opened. The mailbox at the farmhouse has hand-drawn lettering saying "B. Jones 82," a reference to the park's opening in 1982. Then known as EPCOT Center, it was the first theme park opened by Disney which was not a traditional Magic Kingdom, so its turn toward "edutainment" in such attractions as the Land pavilion was a deliberate strategy to imbue the park with an experimental flavor, the better to distinguish it from its Magic Kingdom cousin. Actual trees were used as specific models when creating the molds for the artificial trees in the opening scenes of the boat attraction. The large sycamore outside the farmhouse, for instance, is a duplicate of one standing outside a car wash in Burbank, California—home to the Walt Disney Studios.

Western River Expedition

The mechanized buffalo and prairie dogs in Living with the Land were originally created for a ride in the Magic Kingdom. When the Magic Kingdom first opened, it did not have a long, immersive boat ride with robotic performers. The designers thought there would be no interest in a duplicate of Pirates of the Caribbean from California, since Florida was so close to the real Caribbean. Instead, they designed Western River Expedition, a boat ride through desert buttes and misadventures with all sorts of figures from the Old West. However, visitors asked for Pirates of the Caribbean so often that the Western River Expedition idea was shelved and Pirates of the Caribbean was built instead. The buffalo and prairie dogs, which had already been built, were simply put into storage until they were resurrected at Epcot. Many of the design elements for Western River Expedition ended up being recycled in Big Thunder Mountain Railroad. The Magic Kingdom's version of the ride uses Monument Valley as its stylistic template, which matches the plans for Western River Expedition. In fact, the runaway mine train concept itself started as Thunder Mesa, a mountainous portion of the planned Western River Expedition. The name "Western River" was later used at Tokyo Disneyland, whose river circling the island is called the Western River, and the steam train is labeled the Western River Railroad.

Soarin' Over California

One awkward cut in the preshow video at Soarin' reveals its West Coast origins. Many folks may realize that Soarin' was a transplant from Anaheim's Disney's California Adventure, where it was called Soarin' Over California. The ride showcases only vistas from the Golden State and ends with Disneyland, and the preshow video lists only cities in California. But the host on the video, played by Patrick Warburton, actually mentions the name of the ride: "Hello, and welcome to Soarin'." Visitors paying close attention will realize the actor's mouth shuts unnaturally quickly at the end of this sentence, for this is the result of editing the video and audio away from the original line: "Hello, and welcome to Soarin' Over California."

Former Disney CEO Michael Eisner

The attraction features not only one, but two Hidden Mickeys: the more obvious mouse symbol made out of fireworks recalls the effect seen in Disneyland's then-current nightly fireworks, Believe, and the less-obvious Mickey can only be seen by those with quick eyes, on the golf ball hit toward the screen. The golfer? None other than then-CEO of the Walt Disney Company, Michael Eisner.

Journey into YOUR Imagination

Originally named "Journey into Imagination," the ride was changed in 1999 to "Journey into YOUR Imagination," with entirely new sets and show elements. Figment and Dreamfinder were ditched as hosts of the traditional dark ride, and new ride vehicles were constructed, with a new ride mechanism. The Figment-free show relied heavily on optical illusions such as a cement block falling through a table or a fish swimming out of its tank. Some of the optical illusions remain in the attraction today, such as the butterfly in a cage which disappears as we pass by it, or the upside down room, which originally lacked any wild color schemes. During Figment's absence, he was only represented in the attraction by one clay model in the queue, at the end of the metal shelves. These bits of clay looked unrelated to each other, but when viewed "from the front" they combined to form Figment's familiar head. By 2002, the attraction was renamed back to "Journey into Imagination with Figment," and many show elements that related to the former hosts were returned to the attraction. The obscure Figment tribute, however, remained in the queue.

Dreamfinder

A doorway halfway through Journey Into Imagination with Figment offers tribute to his onetime co-host of the attraction. The sets of the current ride were created for Journey into Your Imagination, a Figment-free attraction that was embellished by adding Figment back into it. But Figment got his start in the original Journey into Imagination ride, where he and the Dreamfinder took visitors through bizarre sets to illustrate the variability of imagination and creativity. The Dreamfinder is now referenced just after the Smell Lab, on a door that is labeled "Dean Finder." Sharp-eyed visitors can spot another reference to the Dreamfinder: the cartoon of Figment seen in his upside-down house includes a segment where Figment dresses up in Dreamfinder's distinctive magician-like red hat and cape.

One Little Spark

The theme song for the original Imagination pavilion is honored in today's attraction. In the climactic scene of the ride, multiple Figment figures are performing various creative activities. Near the center of the set hangs an oversized poster of sheet music for the song "One Little Spark," the theme song of the original version of the ride. An interim update of the attraction that introduced the Imagination Institute without Figment and the Dreamfinder did not play the song, but the modern version of the ride did bring back the melody as an underscore and theme during key moments of the show. The same sheet of music in the finale offers a second nod to the past in the form of a silhouette of the Dream Vehicle—that bulbous contraption that flew through the sky with the aid of a balloon—at the very top of the sheet of music.

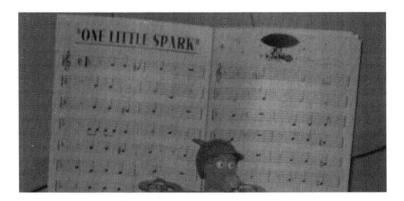

A Trip to the Moon

The last set in Journey Into Imagination with Figment makes reference to the former Horizons pavilion. The video of Dr. Nigel Channing (Eric Idle) as the face of the moon recalls a key moment in Horizons, when the Jules Verne story "From the Earth to the Moon" was showcased as one of the visions of the future. In that scene, an animatronic man is catapulted to the moon in a large bullet, and a snippet of George Melies's 1902 adaptation called *A Trip to the Moon* was also visible nearby, in which the moon's entire surface is covered by a face…and the spaceship-bullet lodges itself in one of its eyes.

The Computer Wore Tennis Shoes

The Imagination attraction incorporates a different tribute as well. An ostensible computer control room for the Imagination Institute pays reference to yet another "mad scientist" movie in Disney's film vault, the 1969 movie *The Computer Wore Tennis Shoes*, featuring Kurt Russell. To honor the movie, the room-sized computer in the Imagination pavilion actually has a pair of shoes at its base, and a letterman jacket from Medford (the college at which the movie takes place) hangs on a nearby peg.

Figment's Place

For a brief time after Figment's return to the Imagination pavilion, the walkaround Figment character was available for a meet-and-greet in the former Kodak shop between the main pavilion and the theater. Figment's Place is now unlabeled, but the décor inside is still visible through the windows.

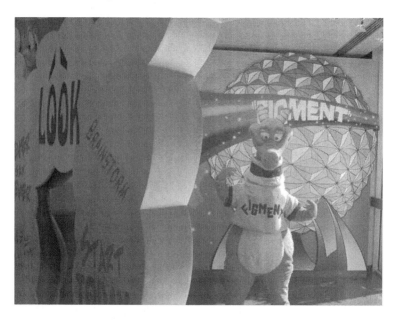

Dream Vehicle

A contraption near the ceiling in MouseGear was a prop used in the original Imagination pavilion. Dreamfinder was seen in the original attraction flying through the sky in the "Dream Vehicle," an elongated bulbous vehicle held aloft by an overhead balloon as it traveled through the skies gathering dreams. The large metallic vehicle used in the attraction is now on display atop a shelf near the ceiling, opposite the cash registers in MouseGear. The original Journey Into Imagination was an Omnimover-type ride, with vehicles first circling a round stage that contained the flying Dream Vehicle before entering the larger, more traditional journey through sets that imaginatively explored numbers, letters, painting, and science.

Epcot's 25th Anniversary

A room in an unused breezeway of Future World was home to Epcot's celebration of its 25th anniversary in 2007. A colorful timeline of the park's history adorns one wall outside of this room still, though the sign announcing the trinket-filled museum inside no longer appears above the doors.

EPCOT Center Logo

In addition to the original pavilions having unique logos, the entire park of EPCOT Center had its own logo, which represented a stylized sphere made up of intersecting ellipses. This symbol is still visible today as an oversized etching in the concrete ground just south of the Fountain of Nations. Also, it can be glimpsed in the metal security gates outside of the baggage check zone of the main entrance.

Lights of Winter

Bolts in the ground demonstrate where an illuminated holiday display was located. Until 2009, the walkway connecting Future World to World Showcase was graced with rows of white arches that played holiday music from loudspeakers overhead. At nighttime, the arches came alive with a multicolored, syncopated light show; the bulbs were made to dance with the music. The Lights of Winter last appeared in 2008. Bolts on the ground on both sides of the walkway, where the arches were affixed each year, are now the only traces remaining.

If You Had Wings

Gran Fiesta Tour honors a former ride in the Magic Kingdom.
Several of the interior scenes of the attraction inside the Mexico
pavilion, Gran Fiesta Tour, are homages to similar moments from a
dark ride in the Magic Kingdom called "If You Had Wings."
Examples include the lakeside temple scenes and cliff divers. Even
the same songwriter, X Atencio, wrote the theme songs for both
attractions. An instrumental version of the theme song from "If You
Had Wings" can still be heard at Cosmic Ray's Starlight Café.

El Rio Del Tiempo

Until its 2007 refurbishment, the Gran Fiesta Tour was known as El Rio Del Tiempo, when it offered a more relaxing journey through Mexico, explicitly pointing out the country's history. For that reason, the initial tunnel was framed by paintings of native peoples. These paintings remain in the modern attraction, although the ride is no longer presented as a historically-informed tour, but rather a search for Donald Duck, so that he can perform at a concert that same evening.

Viking Ship Playground

Pieces of the interactive sets used for the Kim Possible cell-phone game were once used as part of a much larger play area built in the shape of a Viking ship. For many years, visitors could clamor aboard a large wooden vessel, which became mere decoration for a while after access was blocked in 2006. The ship was finally removed in early 2009. There were no traditional play area elements left, save for a small see-saw. After the ship was dismantled, the ornate sea-monster mast was retained for use in the Kim Possible Adventure.

Norway Audio-Animatronics

The molds for many of the Viking figures in Maelstrom came from other Epcot attractions. Although external sculpting was done fresh for the figures, the basic molds for the figures in the Norway pavilion attraction were taken from figures done for Spaceship Earth and World of Motion to save costs, and it didn't hurt that those rides had many dozens of pre-made molds from which to choose.

Rhine River Cruise

A large show building poking out over the embattlements and spires of the Germany pavilion was originally built to house an attraction, a floating journey down the Rhine River. Visitors would have witnessed scenes from the Ruhr valley, picturesque Heidelberg, the moody Black Forest, and the festive Oktoberfest. The entrance to this attraction would have been through an oversized archway now home to a large painted mural.

Never-Built Epcot Pavilions

Remnants of a once-planned Africa pavilion remain between the China and Germany pavilions. The minimal theming done here was simultaneously a test of color and thematic matching with its surroundings and an attempt to entice some African governments to sponsor a pavilion at Epcot. When sponsorship never materialized, the area became a minor shopping and refreshment area. Other planned exhibits include one dedicated to Russia, with enormous onion domes and a ride, and one for Switzerland, which would have brought a version of Disneyland's Matterhorn roller-coaster to Epcot. In all cases, the lack of sufficient sponsorship spelled the end to the projects.

Good Beats

One thatched hut in the unheralded African section of World Showcase still advertises its old line of business. Now used to display hand-carved trinkets, this hut bears a sign atop it proclaiming "Mdundo Kibanda," which is Swahili for "Good Beats." The name makes no sense now, but its meaning snaps into focus if you know that the first occupant of this space used to sell drums instead.

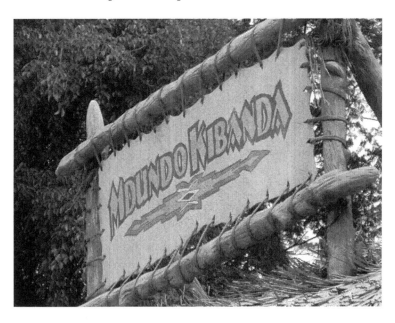

Imagineer Rick Rothschild

Designers of the American Adventure attraction left behind images of themselves. The original show director for the American Adventure, Rick Rothschild, can be found in the attraction's lobby as a silhouette portrait just to the right of the entrance door, though a phony ponytail has been added to his profile. The other silhouette portraits are other Imagineers who worked on the project. They had these silhouettes created at the Magic Kingdom's Main Street store.

Imagineers at Thanksgiving

The painting of a Thanksgiving scene on display in the second floor of the American Adventure lobby, just before entering the theater, was painted by Imagineer Sam McKim to include numerous personalities from Imagineering and his own life. For example, fellow Imagineer Harriet Burns was the model for the mother in the painting, and the boy with the dog is none other than Sam's son Brian.

American Adventure Imagineers

Other Imagineer luminaries can be briefly glimpsed inside the American Adventure attraction itself. Legends John Hench, Marty Sklar, and Randy Bright appear in the painting of the victory parade as spectators on the side of the road. As the camera pans out, first Sklar becomes visible above the flutist, then Hench with one hand raised in the air, and finally Bright, with two hands in the air. All three were involved in the creation of this seminal attraction.

Disneyland's Train Station

The "Two Brothers" song in the American Adventure includes a scene filmed at Disneyland. During the film that plays during the "Two Brothers" song at the American Adventure, a train depot is shown, which actually can be found at Disneyland's Frontierland train station. This set of buildings sits opposite the tracks in Anaheim and functions only as decoration. The "brothers" in question were played by Imagineers John Olson and Jeff Burke.

American Adventure's Third Narrator

The American Adventure show was originally conceived to have three narrators, each one spanning a century of American history. For this reason, Ben Franklin symbolizes the 1700s and Mark Twain the 1800s, but there is no third narrator for the 1900s. Originally, the third narrator was meant to be Will Rogers, but designers realized three was a crowd when it came to narrating the show, and the decision was reached to leave the century unrepresented by a host.

Meet the World and Mt. Fuji

A large show building behind the Japan pavilion was once slated to receive Meet the World, a show like the American Adventure, or as the base for a thrill ride to take place on Mt. Fuji. The ornate castle covers most of the building, but it can be glimpsed looming over the other buildings.

Renault Product Placement

Two flags appearing suddenly at the corners of the *Impressions de France* movie are there to mask a former sponsor of the attraction. Originally, Renault sponsored the attraction and had a prominent product placement appear on the side of the film. When the sponsorship ended, a waving flag was substituted for this entire screen to block out the no-longer-sponsor, and a second flag was added on the other side for symmetry. A similar approach was used in the Timekeeper movie, when Jules Verne zipped around a modern racetrack, and the former sponsor Renault had to be similarly covered up.

Mary Poppins Buildings

The building at the back of the pavilion facing the garden was constructed using blueprints for a building found in the film *Mary Poppins*. Buildings in the United Kingdom pavilion represent different centuries in its history, from the 1500s to the 1800s.

Disney's Hollywood Studios

Sights & Sounds

A marquee on Keystone Clothiers owes its unique shape to a former attraction that operated here for only a year when the park opened in 1989. Called Sights & Sounds, it allowed visitors to create their own music videos (and take them home). The phrase "You oughta be in pictures" now occupies the spot where the store's name was once visible.

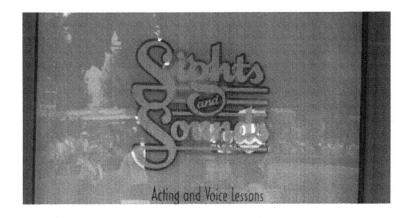

Disney-MGM Studios Logo

The dedication plaque for Disney's Hollywood Studios, located at the end of Hollywood Blvd at the foot of a statue of a filmmaker, not only mentions Disney-MGM Studios by name, but displays the logo as well. The park changed its name in 2008.

Anaheim Produce

The Anaheim Produce stand lives up to its name by selling fruits, but its moniker is also meant as a nod to Disneyland Park, which is located in Anaheim. A sign across the back says "Between Palm and Katella," which is roughly the location of Disneyland (at one time, the part of Harbor Blvd in Anaheim was known as Palm).

Carthay Circle Theater

One shop on Sunset Boulevard replicates the theater which originally premiered Snow White and the Seven Dwarfs. The Once Upon a Time store halfway down the street is reminiscent of the Carthay Circle Theater. That theater in Hollywood held the world premiere in 1937 of *Snow White and the Seven Dwarfs*, and was also the location of the 1929 premiere for the first Silly Symphony, *Skeleton Dance*. A mural inside the Hollywood and Vine restaurant prominently features the Carthay Circle Theater, with *Snow White and the Seven Dwarfs* listed as the marquee film. Other recreations of famous landmarks in Hollywood include the Chinese theater and the Brown Derby restaurant, but almost every structure on Sunset Boulevard and Hollywood Boulevard in the park is modeled on real architecture from greater Los Angeles, not all of it famous.

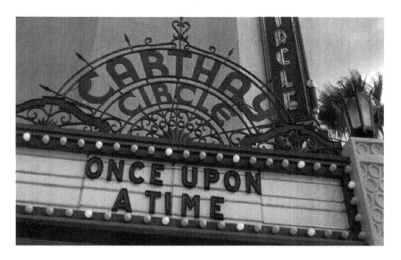

Snow White Premiere

An audio snippet running infrequently in the background music at the Once Upon a Time shop pays homage to the premiere of Disney's first animated feature, *Snow White and the Seven Dwarfs*. This shop in Disney's Hollywood Studios was deliberately constructed as a tribute to that seminal moment in the company's history. The background music stops for a few moments every hour to play an excerpt of the radio coverage of the premiere. Additionally, photographs around the shop capture the night of the premiere and Hollywood celebrities in all their finery.

Sunset Blvd Expansion

The date of the park expansion to include Sunset Blvd. and its attractions, June 1994, is commemorated on the red trolley merchandise cart visible on the street. This trolley bears the number 694 (as in 6/94) as its production number.

Disney's War Effort

Insignia and artwork found at Rosie's All-American Café come from actual art created by the Walt Disney Studios during World War II. Because so many of Walt's animators were called to duty, the studio had to shut down normal production and made war films and patriotic cartoons rather than feature animated movies for a while. Over 1,000 custom insignia for Allied military units were created by a special team within the studios.

Mortimer Mouse

Contractor stamps in the sidewalk of Sunset Boulevard pay respect to Mickey Mouse's original name, Mortimer Mouse. The stamps say "Mortimer & Co. Contractors, 1928"—the same year that Walt Disney lost creative control of Oswald the Lucky Rabbit and created Mickey Mouse instead. A plaque at the FASTPASS machines for Tower of Terror likewise refers to 1928, in this case as the founding

date for Sunset Hills Estates. Other references to 1928 can be seen atop the building at the corner of Hollywood and Sunset and above the restaurant named "Hollywood and Vine." These and many other dates found nearby reinforce the area's theme as

Hollywood set in the late 1920s and early 1930s.

The Twilight Zone

The Tower of Terror includes several references to the television show that inspired its theme, *The Twilight Zone*. Dozens of references scattered around the attraction pay tribute to various episodes of the famous black and white show. In the library, visitors can see a small red machine that answers yes or no questions and a book called *To Serve Man*. Inside the elevator, an inspection certificate is numbered 10259—a reference to the very first airing of the show on October 2, 1959. After the drop, the basement contains still more references to the show, such as a slot machine and a ventriloquist's dummy. Some episodes are even given multiple references. There's one well-known episode called "Time Enough at Last," in which Burgess Meredith's character gets the entire world to himself with no interruptions, and he can finally settle down to read all the books he's wanted to over the years…but almost immediately he breaks his glasses and cannot see. This is referenced twice in the ride; once in the library with a pair of broken glasses, and again in a display case in the exit area of the ride containing personal notices, one of which says "lost—reading glasses, horn rim, thick lenses."

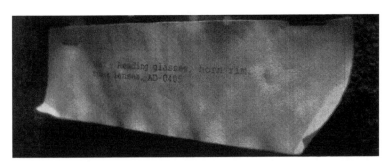

Tower of Terror Hidden Details

The Tower of Terror frequently pays exquisite attention to detail. French bronze statues in the lobby are complimented by authentic antique chairs from the Portuguese Renaissance. There's even a "Hidden Mickey" in the video which explains the attraction in the form of a Mickey Mouse doll held by the little girl authentic to the period, one of the first such dolls ever made in the 1930s. The date of the lightning strike on the building can be found at the entrance gates, which proclaim the order to "keep out" effective on October 31, 1939. The Mah Jongg game in the lobby was played by championship players; designers were so interested in authenticity that professional players were called in to play a game on this board for sixty minutes. At the end of the hour, they simply stood up and left the board as it can be seen today, lending the appearance of both accuracy and sudden disappearance.

Rock 'n' Roller Coaster Imagineers

Disney artists and engineers who designed the Rock 'n' Roller Coaster left behind their initials and birthdays on electrical boxes in the queue area, most notably the dispatch console and a box right at the point where the trains launch. The street address for Walt Disney Imagineering in Glendale (1401 Flower St.) adorns one wall near to that launch point, while the nearby chain-link fences include mention of Buena Vista, which is not only the name of an important Disney subsidiary, but also the street on which the Disney studio first began. Imagineers have a long history of granting themselves immortality in their rides, such as the initials that adorn pipes and crates at the Living Seas. Over at the Sci-Fi Dine-In Restaurant, the license plates on each of the cars indicate initials and birthdays of the Imagineers. The mural depicting San Francisco in the Big City area of Disney's Hollywood Studios likewise shows cars with Imagineers' initials on license plates, though one also uses the initials WDI (Walt Disney Imagineering).

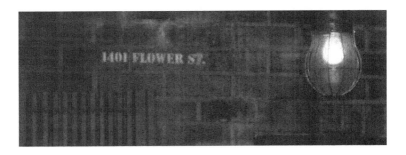

8361 Vine Street

A sign for parking, painted in the bricks above Starring Rolls Café, makes mention of 8361 Vine Street, which is an invented address. Vine is a famous street in Hollywood, but to find 8361 you have to travel to nearby Beverly Blvd in West Hollywood, where the occupant is a coffee shop—not unlike Starring Rolls Café.

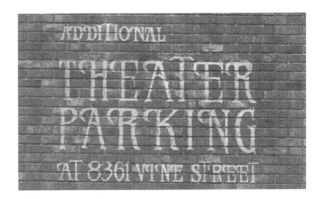

Brown Derby

The famous Wilshire Brown Derby restaurant in California, originator of the Cobb salad, was notable for an oversize structure in front of the building, shaped like an enormous bowler hat. Later, the Hollywood Brown Derby opened across town, absent the bowler hat. The restaurant at Disney's Hollywood Studios reproduces the Hollywood Brown Derby and thus has no bowler structure out front. Nevertheless, Imagineers paid homage to the bowler hat inside the restaurant, courtesy of a distinctively-shaped light fixture.

Early Animation History

The dinosaur standing in the lake in Disney's Hollywood Studios honors the early history of animation. The world's first animated film debuted in 1914, when Windsor McCay released *Gertie the Dinosaur*, a short film in black and white about a sauropod who displays emotions as she interacts with a lake, a sea monster, and a mammoth. In fact, the film was presented as part of a live vaudeville act; McCay would stand on stage in front of the screen and issue instructions to Gertie that she would appear to act upon; at one moment, he tosses an apple to her and then one appears on screen. Before Gertie and this act, McCay had faced an uphill battle with his audiences, who were inclined to believe that drawings could not come to life. Walt's Laugh-O-Grams and Alice Comedies of the 1920s owed much to McCay's innovations, and when Walt later met McCay's son, Walt stressed how much he owed McCay for his trailblazing.

Dip Site #1138

The Oasis Canteen snack stand took on its present name in 2010, but a corner of its menu sign still pays homage to its former identity. Once known as the ~~Dig~~ Dip Site #1138 (the numbers are a reference to THX1138, the first movie by George Lucas), this stand no longer has overt traces of belonging to the Indiana Jones universe. Yet a sign "behind" the menu implies the entire container is a top secret vessel to be stored in a government warehouse, just like the eventual fate of the Ark of the Covenant in the Indiana Jones movies.

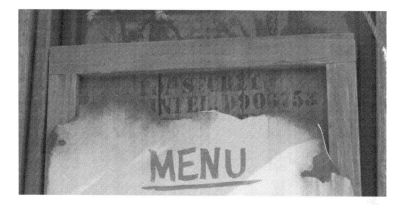

Disney-MGM Imagineers

Mailboxes at the Echo Lake Apartments, between Prime Time Café and Hollywood & Vine restaurant, pay homage to the names of Imagineers who helped build Disney-MGM Studios. Everyone listed in the mailboxes, from John Olson (Field Art Director) to Steve Beyer (Senior Concept Designer) was involved in Disney-MGM Studio's construction. Various job types are represented, encompassing architects, designers, and engineers.

Movie References on Crates

Crates across the lake near the Dockside Diner offer references to famous movies. There's one crate addressed to Rick's Café Americain in *Casablanca*, another to Scarlett O'Hara, one from the Rosebud Sled Company, one earmarked for Max Bialystock, a primary character in *The Producers*, and a final one for George Bailey, the main character from *It's a Wonderful Life*. The name of Min and Bill's Dockside Diner itself is an homage; *Min and Bill* was a 1930 film starring Marie Dressler and Wallace Berry.

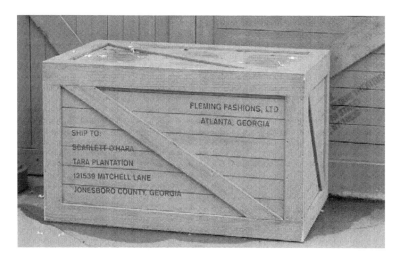

Walt Disney's First Office

A sign in the window above Peevy's Polar Pipeline pays tribute to the start of the Walt Disney company in 1923. This sign advertises "Office Space For Rent," a duplicate of the sign seen by Walt Disney on 4651 Kingswell road in Hollywood, where he found his first office (outside of his garage) in California. Further corroboration comes from the space below. Walt's office had been above the Holly Vermont Realty, and lettering on the door in Disney's Hollywood Studios similarly announces the Holly Vermont Realty.

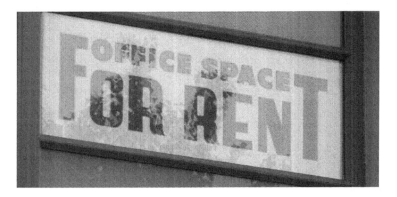

Superstar Television

The home of the American Idol Experience is the Superstar Television Theater, so named to honor the first occupant of this space. Immediately prior to the 2009 opening of the American Idol Experience, this building was known as the ABC Theater and used for tie-in events with the ABC television network. The original attraction here had been Superstar Television, an interactive show that used audience participants to illustrate television and camera effects. After Superstar Television, it was used for Disney's DOUG Live! and Get Happy with ABC.

Chicken Little Sky

The blue sky painting backdrop on the side of one building (visible behind the Brown Derby restaurant) is a remnant of a promotion in 2005 for the *Chicken Little* movie. Prior to this moment, the Stage 5 building had a normal tan color, but to promote the movie and its "sky is falling" message, the cloudscape was painted here with a missing hexagon. When the promotion ended, the sky was retained as a decoration, though it's now whole without a missing hexagon.

Backlot Tour's Original Entrance

The entryway and queue for the Magic of Disney Animation was once used as the entrance for the Backlot tram tour. Until the Backlot Tour moved down the road to the other side of Mickey Avenue (later renamed Pixar Place), this area and its extensive network of switchback-style queue poles held the hundreds of people waiting to board the trams.

Animators at Work

One of the defining features of Disney-MGM Studios was its status as more than a theme park; it was also a working production studio. Accordingly, a highlight of the Magic of Disney Animation building was witnessing animators at work, bent over their desks. The large glass windows used for this viewing remain in the Disney Animation building and form the back wall of a post-show lobby just after the first movie in the attraction. Now tinted to hide the other side, this glass was once transparent and viewers could watch movies such as *Mulan* being created, one cel at a time.

Nine Old Men

Handprints in a central courtyard at Disney Animation come from several of Walt's "Nine Old Men," longtime animators that proved their worth across many projects and decades. Walt's term of endearment is in reference to the "Nine Old Men" traditionally said to populate the Supreme Court. These handprints and signatures were inscribed by the animators themselves during the park's opening in 1989. The names include Marc Davis, Ken Anderson, Ward Kimball, Ollie Johnston, and Frank Thomas.

Hidden Minnie

There's a Hidden Minnie seen in side profile at the Great Movie Ride; she is located in the loading zone, visible as a dark shadow above a gazebo near the center of the mural. The Great Movie Ride is often noted for this use of a Hidden Minnie in the mural at the loading dock, but a more common Hidden Mickey is nearby. Before Sunset Blvd and the sorcerer hat were added, the central plaza was laid out to represent a giant Hidden Mickey seen in profile when viewed from the air, with the theater as part of Mickey's mouth and the round Echo Lake as his ear.

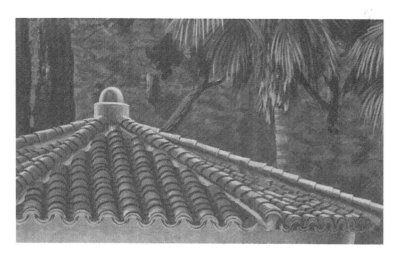

Aliens Tribute

The Great Movie Ride also folds in numerous witticisms in the small print not often read closely. This is most noticeable in the spaceship Nostromo, the section dedicated to the movie *Alien*, where a floor-level monitor off to the left side uses very small typeface to list names of people involved with the movie as well as tongue-in-cheek references to Walt Disney World itself:

- Eric Jacobson - System Alteration Supervisor
- Bob Joslin - Unexplainable Phenomenon Expert
- Glenn Koch - Intergalactic Goo Analyst
- Bob Weis - Spaceship Driver
- Kathy Rogers - Coordination Coordinator
- Brock Thoman - Outer Space Planner
- Doug Esselstrom - Shirt Supervising Officer
- Geoff Puckett - Video Eyewash Designer
- Jack Gillett - Re-Wiring Specialist
- Walt Steel - Technical System Untangler
- Doug Griffith - Still Programming the Witch
- Craig Russell - Everywhere at Once
- John Sullivan - Looking for Ron Beumer
- Tim Kirk - Interior Detail Expert
- Mike Vale - Ear Damage Officer
- Michael Sprout - Operation Manual Re-Writer
- Carol Rotundo - Star Search Astrophysicist.
- Listed as ** MISSING ** are Eric Swapp, Robin Reardon, Cory Sewelson, Ron Beumer, and Paul Osterhaut.

Pharaoh Mickey

Decorative hieroglyphs hidden in the wall of the Great Movie Ride honor Mickey Mouse and Donald Duck. Mickey, dressed as a Pharaoh, is being served food by Donald, shown as a slave, in a stone carving in the Indiana Jones room of the Great Movie Ride, opposite the scene where the Ark of the Covenant is being opened. Set slightly above visitors' heads, this block is seldom noticed unless sought directly. It can be seen to the left of the ride vehicle, after passing the second Anubis statue and in the corner of the room, about halfway up the wall.

Hieroglyphic Droids

Part of the decorations elsewhere in the same room is a tribute to
R2-D2 and C3PO, the droid partnership from the Star Wars movies.
They are drawn as symbolic hieroglyphic symbols, rather than more
direct representations like Mickey and Donald. The connection with
Indiana Jones is a fairly direct one, since George Lucas was the
creative force behind both franchises. The hieroglyphic droids can
be found at eye level, in the middle of the room on the left side.

Tarzan as a Pirate

The swinging Tarzan in the Great Movie Ride was duplicated for
Disneyland Paris. When building the French version of Pirates of
the Caribbean, designers wanted to inject additional excitement into
the attraction in the form of sets and elements not found in the
American versions of the ride. One such innovation was a pirate
swinging from a rope right over the boat full of Guests. The Tarzan
figure from the Great Movie Ride provided a ready-made mold for
the Paris attraction; they merely had to change the costume and
duplicate the figure.

Casablanca Plane

The plane in the background of the *Casablanca* set of the Great
Movie Ride is not from the movie, yet has its own interesting tale.
Persistent urban legend claims that the plane used in this set comes
from the movie *Casablanca*, but there is conclusive evidence that no
real plane was used in shooting that scene, and they used a mock-up
instead that was smaller in scale. Disney purchased a full-sized, real
Lockheed plane for the Great Movie Ride. The back half of the
Disney's Lockheed was put to use elsewhere in the property, in the
Magic Kingdom's Jungle Cruise. This prop can be seen near the
animatronic of the elephant and the African savannah.

Wizard of Oz Tornado

The fans and swirling visuals during the Sorcerer Mickey portion of
the Great Movie Ride were originally created to approximate being
inside a tornado, meant as an introduction to the Wizard of Oz set
that followed. The transition to a crashed house, complete with
crushed witch below, would have been complete if this section were
themed to the tornado, but contract negotiations with MGM
dictated that the Wizard of Oz sequence not last three sets, but only
two. As a result, the already-built first set was repurposed for the
Sorcerer's Apprentice scene.

Space Mountain's Old Preshow

One scene in the movies of the Sci-Fi Dine-In Theater was also once
part of Space Mountain. A humanoid robot named Garco makes a
brief appearance in a montage of old film clips in the Sci-Fi Drive-In
Theater, but he had once also appeared in "Space Mountain TV," a
video in the queue of Space Mountain that showed ostensible
channel-surfing through FedEx commercials and whimsical news
shows. There identified as Galactic President Garco, he actually
traces his lineage on film to a 1957 episode of the show
"Disneyland," on an episode called "Mars and Beyond" that
postulated life on Mars. That queue video at Space Mountain was
rife with references to old Disney properties. One could glimpse the
ship from Flight of the Navigator, visible when Crazy Larry tried to

sell used spaceships. Crazy Larry was himself famous in Disney circles: the actor was Charles Fleischer, voice of Roger Rabbit. There was a Hidden Mickey in the form of a satellite unfurling radio antenna ears, as well as a tribute to the old ride Mission to Mars, in the form of a downward view of a rocket launching that was once part of the attraction.

Disney-MGM Studios Name

The original name of Disney's Hollywood Studios, Disney-MGM Studios, was changed in 2008. At that time, signs all over the park were repainted. Only two signs eluded detection: most of the black spray-paint stencil signs on the walls in Writer's Stop were rubbed out and replaced with "Disney's Hollywood Studios," but two such stencil signs were left unmolested as "Disney-MGM Studios"—one behind the cash register, and one at the barstool counter, below counter level.

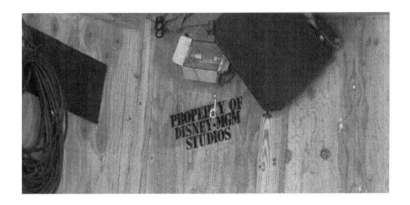

Walt's Subway

The subway lines, listed as supposedly running below the Big City/Streets of America facades, honor Walt Disney by using "W" and "D" as the names of the subway lines. This part of the set is meant to represent New York, which like many cities around the world uses letters for subway routes. But there are no real W or D lines in New York.

Radio Disney

When Disney's Hollywood Studios (then Disney-MGM Studios) first opened in 1989, it held working production facilities and soundstages, not just to simulate but actually to be a working studio. As part of this effort, Disney's then-new radio network called Radio Disney was given production space next to Sounds Dangerous. While signs on the windows remain (now proclaiming WDW Radio Studio), the facility has been vacant for some years.

Indiana Jones Movie Props

Life-sized vehicle props at the exit to the Indiana Jones Epic Stunt Spectacular were taken from the third movie, *Indiana Jones and the Last Crusade*. The flat bed truck and the distinctive tank, while appearing now in a state of advanced decrepitude after a long stint exposed to the elements, are the same vehicles used in the filming of the movie.

Horizons Mold

A mold for a vehicle once used at Epcot's Horizons can be seen at the Backlot Express restaurant. Atop one corner of the dining area in this restaurant is the mold used to create a hovercraft used in Horizons, the original pavilion to occupy the spot now taken by Mission: Space. Horizons celebrated the "future that never was," with often quirky visions of the future which never came to pass. The hovercraft was located in the foreground of a scene where oranges were being harvested by remote-controlled vehicles. A robotic butler sporting many arms was another iconic scene from Horizons that manages to resurface as part of a video every so often somewhere in the Disney park empire. Disneyland's Innoventions flashes an image of the robotic butler, for instance, as did the "One Man's Dream" movie that Disneyland opened in its Opera House to celebrate its Golden Anniversary in 2005.

MuppetVision Preshow

A few of the marching soldiers that appear in MuppetVision 3-D can be seen in the ceiling of the preshow area. The preshow is home to numerous inside jokes, such as the spaceship Swine Trek used in "Pigs in Space," a picture of Muppet creator Jim Henson, and even a Hidden Bunsen Honeydew and Beaker (represented as a ball with glasses and a whistle with bulging eyes). Inside the theater itself are further gags, such as the sheet music in front of the penguin orchestra—it's the music for "The Rainbow Connection," a song that appeared in the first Muppet Movie. In typical Muppet style, there are also puns and wordplays scattered about the attraction. The preshow sports a net full of jello (spoken aloud, it sounds like Annette Funicello), as well as a crate labeled 2-D Fruities (i.e., "tutti frutties"). The projector inside the auditorium is labeled as a Yell & Howell model, which is simultaneously a play on words ("yell and howl") and a reference to a prominent manufacturer of projectors named Bell and Howell.

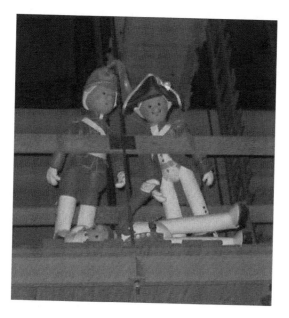

Muppet Movie Props

Set pieces reproduced in the Stage 1 Company Store, a shop near MuppetVision, include the lobby of Happiness Hotel (from *The Great Muppet Caper*) and the lockers doubling as micro-apartments (from *The Muppets Take Manhattan*). Look up high for cutout flats of a bus and a delivery truck, from the Muppet-produced musical "Manhattan Melodies", part of *The Muppets Take Manhattan*.

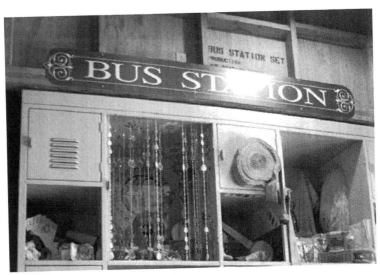

Roger Rabbit Ride

The building at the exit to Backlot Tour was so themed because this area was once slated to receive a *Who Framed Roger Rabbit* makeover. Due to this connection, the term ACME is used several times in this store. In that cartoon universe, ACME is considered a generic but ubiquitous name. The Roger Rabbit expansion was once set for the end of Sunset Boulevard and would have included a ride on flight simulators called Toontown Trolley, a dark ride called Baby Herman's Runaway Baby Buggy Ride, and Benny the Cab, the dark ride that later became Roger Rabbit's CarToon Spin at Disneyland. This expansion of "Roger Rabbit's Hollywood" was to have been part of the "Disney Decade" of expansion at the theme parks, which would have included a land behind Main Street in Disneyland, Westcot duplicating Epcot in Anaheim, and a Beauty and the Beast

dark ride at the Magic Kingdom. Creative differences between
Disney and the other respective owners of the Roger Rabbit
property meant development never got off the ground, and only the
warehouse remained. There is also a glass window near Echo Lake
that recalls a scene in which Roger crashes through a window
leaving only his outline behind. Another nearby sign in Echo Lake
advertises Eddie Valiant, his co-star. A further reference to Roger
Rabbit can be found in the Toon Patrol car used in the movie, now
housed at the Backlot Express restaurant dining area. Elsewhere at
Backlot Express is the stripped-down chassis of the vehicle that was
used to film sequence for Benny the Cab. Some sort of vehicle
platform had to be physically present to hold the live-action actors,
but because most of the car was later animated over the filmed
portion, it lacks a roof and sides.

Mighty Ducks Mask

High in the rafters of the ACME Warehouse, a shop opposite the Studio Catering Company restaurant, is an unassuming prop in the form of a white hockey mask, with familiar duck bill. This unique shape is recognizable as the trademark for the Mighty Ducks of Anaheim, the professional hockey team founded by Disney and sold in 2005. Disney had based the name on a 1992 movie, *The Mighty Ducks.* A few years after its sale, the team changed its name simply to the Ducks.

Residential Street

The Residential Street movie sets were dismantled in 2004, but a brief view of them can be seen in the men's restroom adjacent to the entrance for the Backlot Tour. There, framed photographs on the tiled wall show Residential Street, as well as the Big City area when it was used for filming. Residential Street was famous as the location of the house façade used in the *Golden Girls* TV show, as well as the original home of the Osborne Family Spectacle of Lights. Residential Street was removed and demolished to make room for the amphitheater for Lights, Motors, Action, which opened in 2005.

World of Motion Props

Some of the props in the warehouse at the Backlot Tour came from the former attraction World of Motion. The warehouse is used as a queue for visitors waiting to board the trams, and it is crammed full of props used in movies, as well as several artifacts from Epcot's former ride World of Motion, which celebrated the history of transportation. Of particular interest are several robotic performers, now unplugged and stripped of their clothing. Examples include a balloonist, a man strapped to a wooden wing, and a collection of several masks used to give Audio-Animatronics their realistic faces.

Main Street Antiques

While some of the movie props in the warehouse are highly recognizable, such as the rocket backpack from *The Rocketeer* and the taxi cab used in *The Great Muppet Caper*, most of the artifacts appear unremarkable. Yet several are recycled objects from Walt Disney World's history; hitching posts and antique mutoscopes transported from the Magic Kingdom's Main Street welcome visitors to the warehouse, for instance, and banners used in World of Motion adorn one wall.

Walt's Airplane

The plane visible on the Backlot Tour is the very one used by Walt Disney to scout the then-undeveloped Walt Disney World property. "Mickey Mouse One," as the plane was called in reference to the presidential plane Air Force One, is a Grumman G-159 Gulfstream I multi-engine propeller plane built in 1963. It was used by Walt Disney and later executives as a corporate aircraft, until it was finally decommissioned in the late 1980s and retired to Disney's Hollywood Studios. While Orlando's main airport saw Mickey Mouse One with regularity, after a while it made sense for Disney to build an airstrip right on Walt Disney World property. Although the idea had been to cater to visitors flying with small commercial airlines from regional airports, Disney's airstrip was never heavily used, as it functioned only as an "uncontrolled" landing strip and could not store many planes. Plans for a Disney-built, wide-winged plane designed for this type of short-takeoff runway (STOLport) never came to fruition, and the airstrip fell into disuse. To this day, the remnants of the airstrip can still be found to the east of the toll booths at the Magic Kingdom's parking lot.

PIXAR Director Pete Docter

The director of Monsters Inc. is given a tribute at the meet-and-greet location near the Backlot Tour. Handwritten notes on Walt Disney Entertainment letterhead are signed "Pete D" and remind employees of apparently recent policies, such as to avoid jokes about Jonas since they are "too easy." Jonas is a nod to PIXAR employee Jonas Rivera, who was the producer of *Up* (2009).

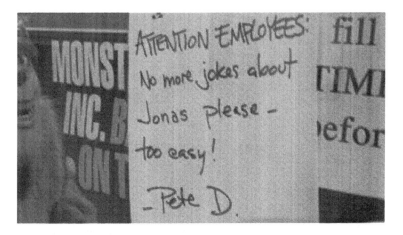

PIXAR Corporate Logos

The queue for Toy Story Midway Mania contains two side-by-side references to PIXAR. Flanking the *Audio-Animatronics* Mr. Potato Head barker are the two main symbols of the innovative studio—a ball with a distinctive star pattern can be seen on one side (known as the Luxo ball), while the other side has the desk lamp (named Luxo Jr.) seen bouncing around in the corporate logo before every PIXAR movie. The ball is again seen at the end of the ride, visible on one wall just before disembarking.

Toy Story Mania Single Rider Line

The Toy Story Midway Mania marquee retains traces of a single-rider line that was only in use for a few months when the ride was new. Two small, blank rectangular signs near the bottom of the attraction's FASTPASS return sign were installed to cover up the "&" symbol and the words "Single Riders." Originally, single riders were allowed in the FASTPASS return line with no tickets, but this proved unworkable operationally in the long run, and the option was discontinued without major adjustment to the attraction's sign.

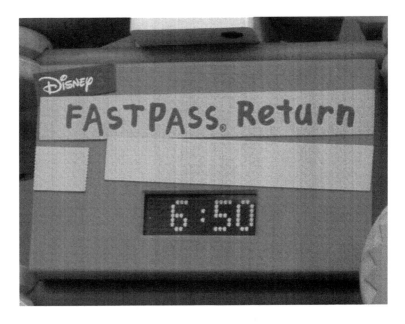

Animator Joe Ranft

One blue "book" spine in the FASTPASS queue for Toy Story Midway Mania pays tribute to longtime PIXAR animator, Joe Ranft, who died in 2005 in an automobile accident. Ranft is the ostensible author of this blue "book," which is named *Magic Made Easy*, in deference to Ranft's abilities as an amateur magician.

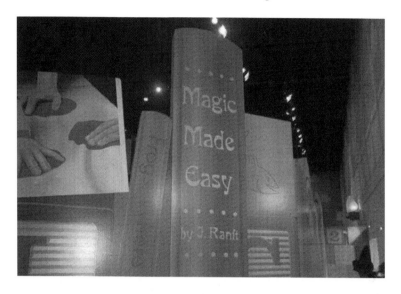

Imagineer John Lasseter

The chief creative officer of PIXAR as well as a prominent figure in Walt Disney Imagineering, John Lasseter is often associated with his 1988 short *Tin Toy*, the first completely computer animated short. It comes as no surprise that we see the Golden Books version of this famous story as we exit Toy Story Mania. Sharp-eyed visitors can even spy Lasseter's name, given as the ostensible author of a different green book, seen painted on the wall at the end of the ride. The book Lasseter supposedly wrote? *Tin Toy*, of course. The idea of toys being alive in that story provided Lasseter with the germ of the concept which would later become *Toy Story*, so *Tin Toy*'s presence in the *Toy Story* attraction makes sense.

Backstage Pass

Skywalk bridges connecting soundstages in PIXAR Place are remnants of the original Backlot Tour. When the park first opened, the tram tour was followed by a walking tour of several soundstages on what is now PIXAR Place, and guests transitioned between buildings on the bridges. This part of the tour was later made its own attraction called Backstage Pass, until it closed in 2001 to open up areas of the park to the general flow of visitors.

Disney's Animal Kingdom

Discovery River Boat Tour

Docks on either side of Discovery Island were once used for boats that transported guests around the park's waterways. Originally known as the Discovery River Boat Tour, this attraction suffered long lines and little to look at, so by the end of 1998 it was renamed the Discovery River Taxis, to point out that its function was transportation. That too did not grab the public's attention, and for most of 1999 it was known as the Radio Disney River Cruise, aimed at younger audiences, until it finally closed for good in August 1999. The five boats in the fleet (Crocodile Belle, Darting Dragonfly, Hasty Hippo, Leaping Lizard, and Otter Nonsense) cruised past a few points of interest, like frothy bubbles near Africa meant to imply an underwater creature, or a full-size animated Iguanodon standing in shallow water near Dinoland, USA. The boats can sometimes be seen today transporting a live band playing amplified music in the Asia/Dinoland lagoon.

Beastlie Kingdomme

A solitary stone dragon visible from the bridge to Camp Minnie-Mickey honors a onetime idea for a new land. Beastlie Kingdomme, a land of mythical creatures that never lived, was meant to be built near here in the area now occupied by Camp Minnie-Mickey, but the idea lost out to the need for more children's areas in the park. Land was set aside on the other side of Camp Minnie-Mickey, which was conceived with an Adirondack theme to blend more naturally into the fantasy realm, should that ever be built. When the Discovery River Boat Tour was transporting visitors around the park's waterways, the stone dragon was one of the primary show elements, spewing flames each time a boat came close.

Dragon Benches

Dragon designs on benches throughout the park make reference to
Beastlie Kingdomme. Dragons were part of the original plan for
expansion of this park right from the beginning. To this day, the
official logo for Disney's Animal Kingdom features a dragon
silhouette as part of the Tree of Life; this logo can be seen
throughout the park on trash cans and other locations. The
dedication plaque for Disney's Animal Kingdom, located in the Oasis
section of the park, mentions dragons too. Even the ticket booths in
front of the park made reference to the original plan to build the
park's thematic foundation on the triumvirate of real animals,
prehistoric ones, and imaginary ones. A carved representation of an
elephant's head adorns the roof of one ticket booth, with a second
booth hosting a triceratops, and the third home to a dragon's head.

Lion King Puppets

The minimally-animated, oversized puppets in the Festival of the Lion King came from Disneyland. A former daytime street parade named the Lion King Celebration at Disneyland featured the giraffe, elephant, Simba, and Pumbaa that now form the centerpieces of the large float units for the show in Disney's Animal Kingdom. There is a long tradition of re-using parade elements in a more permanent fashion whenever possible. For instance, the golden camels that today spit water at the Magic Carpets of Aladdin come from a parade at Disney's Hollywood Studios called Aladdin's Royal Caravan, after also serving a stint at the Soundstage restaurant after the parade's end.

Jane Goodall's Chimp

A prominent sculpture of a chimpanzee on the Tree of Life owes its existence to biologist Jane Goodall's visit to the park. During construction of Disney's Animal Kingdom, famous researcher Jane Goodall viewed the Tree of Life and wondered why there was no chimp prominently represented. Given a chance to remedy that, she chose David Graybeard, a chimpanzee she had known for a long time, to immortalize near the entrance to It's Tough to be a Bug, and a plaque was placed nearby to explain Graybeard's significance.

Original Kilimanjaro Safari Storyline

A character named Dr. Catherine Jobson in the queue video of Kilimanjaro Safari is a remnant of a different storyline for this attraction from its opening until 2007, when Dr. Jobson's role in the attraction was removed. Previously, her voice was heard in the safari truck, since she was supposedly traveling overhead by plane with warden Wilson. She informed the audience of the death of the elephant matriarch Big Red, shot by poachers, and the disappearance of her offspring Little Red. The safari truck helped corner the poachers and recover Little Red.

Catherine Jobson Ph.D.
Wildlife Researcher

Gorilla Falls

The original name of the Pangani Forest walking trail, Gorilla Falls, can still be seen on a crate near the gorilla observation area. This crate makes mention of the Gorilla Falls Conservation School. For those seeking a true intercultural connection, look for a reference to the same title in Swahili near the entrance to the walking trail.

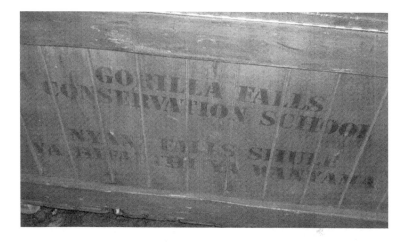

Disney's Animal Kingdom's Chief Designer

The Imagineer in charge of Disney's Animal Kingdom, Joe Rohde, is portrayed throughout Africa on weather-worn posters plastered to the outside of several buildings. Rohde is shown as a drawing of "Captain Bob", who advertises balloon rides over the safari. Those seeking closure and for the theming to come full-circle will revel in the discovery of an actual parachute, meant to be Captain Bob's, in the ceiling of the queue of Kilimanjaro Safari.

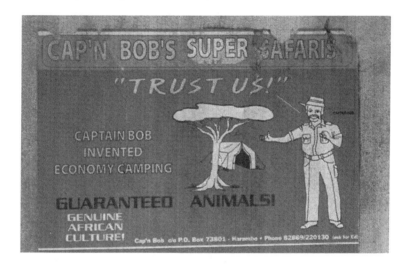

Disney Executive Frank Wells

One photograph in the FASTPASS queue for Expedition Everest shows former Disney executive Frank Wells near the base camp of Mt. Everest. An avid mountain climber, Wells had wanted to conquer the tallest mountain in all seven continents, which is why he is honored on the Magic Kingdom's Main Street windows with the phrase "Seven Summits Expedition." Wells succeeded on six of the seven continents; his two attempts to make it to the summit of Everest were unsuccessful. There is also a tribute to Wells in Disneyland's Matterhorn, where climbing gear is stamped "Wells Expedition" on one box.

Chakranadi Chicken Shop

The addition in 2007 of Yak and Yeti heralded the first table-service restaurant in the park, which took the place of two quick-service locations, Sunaulo Toran Fries and Chakranadi Chicken Shop. One ornate wall of the distinctively-themed Chakranadi Chicken Shop was retained for the outdoor courtyard of the Yak and Yeti's counter-service operation, forging a link to the former inhabitant of this space.

Werikhe Way

A sign on Yak and Yeti proclaims it to be located at 775 Werikhe Way, a street whose name is an homage to the Kenyan conservationist Michael Werikhe (1956-1999). Known in some circles as the "Rhino Man," Werikhe achieved fame by making long fundraising walks to generate awareness of the plight of black rhinos, whose numbers were in rapid decline. By honoring Werikhe, park designers hew closely to the park's theme of conservation and preservation.

Disney's Animal Kingdom Opening Year

Highway signs in Chester and Hester's Dino-Rama honor the opening date of Disney's Animal Kingdom. Two signs label the main curving road of the land as Highway 498, which reference the opening date of Disney's Animal Kingdom on April 22, 1998. One sign sits near the Boneyard play area, while the other can be found near the road's dead-end alongside Primeval Whirl. A third reference to highway 498 can be seen off to the side of the large Dinosaur billboard at the very end of the road. A dedication plaque just outside the entrance to the Dino Institute makes a reference to April 22, 1978—a tribute to April 22, 1998, the day that Disney's Animal Kingdom opened. This portion of the institute is meant to portray an old-fashioned (and now out-dated) museum, and placing its supposed birth in the 1970s adds weight to the fiction.

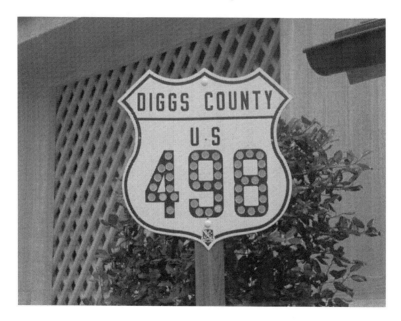

Dinoland, U.S.A. Backstory

The nearby fake gas pump, once located outside but now found inside the store, provides the key to Dinoland U.S.A.'s entire theme. The backstory to the land begins with Chester and Hester, who owned a sleepy gas station when dinosaur bones were discovered in the nearby archeological dig. The success of that dig led scientists to take over a shack and expand it with their trailers; this is now known as Restaurantosaurus. The huge fossil dig also lured a modern museum, which houses the ride Dinosaur. Due in part to all their new neighbors and the traffic they attracted, Chester and Hester found it more profitable to sell dino trinkets to visitors than gas, so they converted their store. As sales soared, they expanded into the nearby "parking lot" and built midway games and carnival rides to entertain the travelers. Chester and Hester are displayed on a photo inside Restaurantosaurus.

Disney's Animal Kingdom Outline

The giant stegosaurus shoulder bone used to create the sign for the Boneyard is actually an outline of the original shape of Disney's Animal Kingdom. Before Asia was added, the park had a decidedly elongated shape, with a hump off to one side for Camp Minnie-Mickey. An "N" with an arrow on one side of the calcified marquee orients the viewer toward the north, and the bone's shape suddenly makes sense as the park's original outline. The Boneyard is site of an archeological dig by several professors and their students. Dr. Bernard Dunn, Dr. Shirley Woo, and Dr. Eugene McGee are joined by students Jenny Weinstein, Mark "Animal" Rios, and Sam Gonzales. Many of their stories can be read in bits and pieces in letters displayed in the dining rooms of Restaurantosaurus.

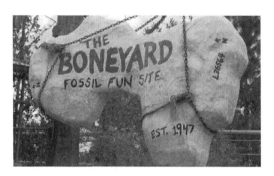

Former DVC Sales Outpost

Now used as a stopover point in parkwide quests and games for children, the hut between the Boneyard and Restaurantosaurus was once home to the Disney Vacation Club, where visitors could obtain general information about sales of the Disney timeshare company. One tidbit from the earlier resident remains; a crate just outside the hut is labeled "Ship to Disney's Old Key West Resort," in reference to one of the earliest DVC properties at Walt Disney World, Old Key West.

Imagineer Joe Rohde

The chief designer of Disney's Animal Kingdom has a subtle tribute at the Kid's Discovery station in Dinoland U.S.A., where the crate of bones is labeled "RD-1 Field Sample." That can be read aloud as "roadie" (if interchanging the "1" for an "I" as often happens in text messaging), which is the correct pronunciation of Rohde's last name. A less permanent homage to Rohde was previously scrawled in permanent marker on a blue barrel near Expedition Everest when Anandapur was first created.

Primeval World

Just inside the main dining room at Restaurantosaurus is a photo of Walt Disney with the dinosaurs from a 1964 World's Fair attraction. This is the same ride that eventually gave rise to the Primeval World addition of the Disneyland Railroad. Along the same wall, close to the restrooms, are line drawings from the Rite of Spring section of *Fantasia*, which famously staged a fight between an allosaurus and a stegosaurus and was eventually the inspiration for the climax of the Primeval World attraction as well. That same scene is reproduced in the main hall on a different wall, this time in the same pastel colors as the finished movie. It's also visible as a photograph on the wall in the gift shop at Dino-Rama.

CTX

The attraction now known as Dinosaur was originally called Countdown to Extinction, and abbreviated CTX. The attraction was largely the same experience with a slightly different theme. Markings on the walls and vehicles in Dinosaur pay tribute to the attraction's first name. Parts of the walls and vehicles are still marked "CTX" in reference to the original name of the ride, and numerous references to extinction along the walls of the queue and shop at the exit also pay testament to the ride's original name. One sign on the wall as the ride starts reads WDI-AK98, which gives tribute to Walt Disney Imagineering and the park's opening year of 1998.

Countdown to Extinction Map

A map of the land located opposite Dino Dig still refers to the attraction building as Countdown to Extinction, not Dinosaur. It reads: "You must go here! It is seriously great!! At COUNTDOWN TO EXTINCTION, they actually send you BACK IN TIME to see LIVE DINOSAURS!! For real!!!" Over in Restaurantosaurus, a faux newspaper article next to the ordering stations not only shows the blueprint for the time rover, it mentions T-shirts emblazoned with "I survived extinction!", which made more sense when the ride was still called Countdown to Extinction.

Dinoland U.S.A.'s Former Sponsor

Certain symbols in the ceiling at Dinosaur pay tribute to the original sponsor of the entire land. Pipes located overhead in several locations in the loading zone are labeled with the chemical formulas for ketchup, mustard, and mayonnaise, with even the pipes colored red, yellow, and white to further the gag. The reference to condiments honors McDonald's 1998-2008 sponsorship of the entire Dinoland USA region of the park. References to the food chain were common throughout the land. Food and drink containers with McDonald's logos were left, as if discarded, in places like the Boneyard's upstairs archeology office and the back seat of the "road trip" car near Dino-Rama. There were also McDonald's references alongside the model train in the ceiling of Chester and Hester's Dinosaur Treasures.

Toasters on Dinosaur

The time travel corridors in Dinosaur are scaled-up versions of heating coils from toasters. Disney designers always make a scale model of an attraction before building it; the innards of toasters were used in making the scale model of the two time-travel corridors, and the look of the actual ride was simply copied from the model. Strobe lights and sparks that accompany the effect were inspired by cigarette lighters, simply scaled up twenty times.

General Walt Disney World

Lagoon Wave Machine

Early Walt Disney World executives wanted "the Vacation Kingdom" to feature amenities unique in the world, so they built a wave machine below the Seven Seas Lagoon in order to generate excitement along the beaches of the Polynesian Resort. It never really worked as desired, however, because the waves rapidly eroded the beaches at the Polynesian. The machinery went silent not too long after its first use, but it remains at the bottom of the lagoon, not too far offshore from the Polynesian Resort.

Discovery Island

The island in the middle of Bay Lake (which is not a man-made lake) was once used as a separate attraction at Walt Disney World celebrating close encounters with exotic animals, especially birds. It had previously had light pirate theming and was known as Blackbeard's Island and Treasure Island, until 1977 when it became a wildlife mini-park. Discovery Island closed a year after Disney's Animal Kingdom opened in 1998.

River Country

An overgrown series of slides adjacent to Fort Wilderness was once a water park called River Country. The idea to capture an old-fashioned "watering hole" drew a healthy stream of visitors for many years, but after Blizzard Beach joined Typhoon Lagoon as even-larger water parks on Disney's roster, River Country closed forever.

Walt Disney World Executive Jack Olsen

Cap'n Jack's Restaurant is not named after Captain Jack Sparrow from the Pirates of the Caribbean movies, but Jack Olsen, one of the vice-presidents of Walt Disney World when the Marketplace (then called Disney Village) was originally created. Similarly, a shop called Sir Edwards was named after another vice-president.

Alien Encounter

One room-sized video game, almost a ride, at DisneyQuest takes place in the same fictional universe as the former Magic Kingdom ride, the ExtraTERRORestrial Alien Encounter. This video game, called Invasion, places riders inside an oversized, spider-like planetary crawler called X-S 5000. The experience explicitly mentions its origins from the company X-S Tech, the same company supposedly responsible for the ExtraTERRORestrial Alien Encounter.

Former Ticket Booth

The bridge at Fulton's Crab House ends at an unused booth that looks like a guard shack. This structure is a remnant of Pleasure Island's earlier roots as a restricted-admission zone. All access to the island was controlled and required separate admission tickets, which were sold by this booth.

Fort Wilderness Train

Some paths at Fort Wilderness were once home to the narrow-gauge railroad at the resort. The locomotive once used here was involved in a complex series of trades to finally grant Disneyland a fifth engine, the Ward Kimball.

The Gully Whumper Keel Boat

The Mike Fink Keel Boats, which until 1997 whipped around the Rivers of America, are honored in the Trail's End restaurant at Fort Wilderness. There are small-scale models of keel boats in display boxes that provide an indirect link, but a more direct homage can be found in a piece of the Gully Whumper boat itself from the Magic Kingdom.

Colonel's Cotton Mill

The cotton flower visible on the large mural at the Riverside Mill is a remnant of the time when this restaurant was known as Colonel's Cotton Mill, and the entire resort was called Dixie Landings. When Port Orleans expanded in 2002 to encompass Dixie Landings (then renamed to Port Orleans Riverside), the Colonel's Cotton Mill became the Riverside Mill.

Attraction Dates

Current Attractions

Astro Orbiter (1994-present)

Barnstormer at Goofy's Wiseacre Farm (1996-present)

Big Thunder Mountain Railroad (1975-present)

Buzz Lightyear's Space Ranger Spin (1998-present)

Carousel of Progress (1975-present)

Country Bear Jamboree (1971-present)

Donald's Boat (1996-present)

Dumbo the Flying Elephant (1971-present)

Enchanted Tiki Room Under New Management (1998-present)

Hall of Presidents (1971-present)

Haunted Mansion (1971-present)

It's a Small World (1971-present)

Jungle Cruise (1971-present)

Liberty Square Riverboat / Liberty Belle (1996-present)

Mad Tea Party (1971-present)

Magic Carpets of Aladdin (2001-present)

Main Street Vehicles (1971-present)

Many Adventures of Winnie the Pooh (1999-present)

Mickey's Country House (1988-present)

Mickey's Philharmagic (2003-present)

Minnie's Country House (1988-present)

Monsters, Inc. Laugh Floor (2007-present)

Tomorrowland Transit Authority PeopleMover (1975-present)

Peter Pan's Flight (1971-present)

Pirates of the Caribbean (1973-present)

Prince Charming Regal Carrousel (2010-present)

Snow White's Scary Adventures (1971-present)

Space Mountain (1975-present)

Splash Mountain (1992-present)

Stitch's Great Escape (2004-present)

Swiss Family Treehouse (1971-present)

Tom Sawyer Island (1973-present)

Tomorrowland Speedway (1971-present)

Walt Disney World Railroad (1971-present)

American Adventure (1982-present)
Captain EO (1986-1994; 2010-present)
Circle of Life: An Environmental Fable (1995-present)
Ellen's Energy Adventure (1996-present)
Gran Fiesta Tour (2007-present)
Impressions de France (1982-present)
Innoventions (1994-present)
Journey into Imagination with Figment (2002-present)
Living with the Land (1993-present)
Maelstrom (1988-present)
Mission Space (2003-present)
O Canada (1982-present)
Reflections of China (2003-present)
Seas with Nemo and Friends (2006-present)
Soarin' (2005-present)
Spaceship Earth (1982-present)
Turtle Talk with Crush (2004-present)
Test Track (1999-present)

American Idol Experience (2008-present)
Backlot Tour (1989-present)
Beauty and the Beast Live on Stage (1991-present)
Fantasmic! (1998-present)
Great Movie Ride (1989-present)
Honey I Shrunk the Kids Movie Set Adventure (1990-present)
Indiana Jones Epic Stunt Spectacular (1989-present)
Journey into Narnia (2008-present)
Lights Motors Action (2005-present)
Magic of Disney Animation (2003-present)
MuppetVision 3-D (1991-present)
One Man's Dream (2001-present)
Playhouse Disney Live (2001-present)
Rock 'n Roller Coaster (1999-present)
Sounds Dangerous (1999-present)
Star Tours (1989-present)
Tower of Terror (1994-present)
Toy Story Midway Mania (2008-present)
Voyage of the Little Mermaid (1992-present)

Dinosaur (2000-present)
Expedition Everest (2006-present)
Festival of the Lion King (1998-present)
Finding Nemo – The Musical (2006-present)
Flights of Wonder (1998-present)
It's Tough to be a Bug (1998-present)
Kali River Rapids (1999-present)
Kilimanjaro Safari (1998-present)
Primeval Whirl (2002-present)
Rafiki's Planet Watch (1999-present)
TriceraTop Spin (2001-present)

Former Attractions

20,000 Leagues Under the Sea (1971-1994)
ABC Sound Studio (1997-1999)
America the Beautiful (1975-1984)
American Journeys (1984-1994)
Backstage Pass (1990-2001)
Bear in the Big Blue House (2000-2001)
Cinderella's Golden Carrousel (1971-2010)
CommuniCore (1982-1994)
Conservation Station (1998-1999)
Countdown to Extinction (1998-2000)
Country Bear Christmas Special (1984-2006)
Country Bear Vacation Hoedown (1986-2001)
Davy Crockett Explorer Canoes (1971-1994)
Diamond Horseshoe Jamboree (1986-1995)
Diamond Horseshoe Revue (1971-1986)
Diamond Horseshoe Saloon Revue (1995-2003)
Dick Tracy Diamond Double-Cross (1990-1991)
Discovery Island (1977-1998)
Disney's DOUG Live! (1999-2001)
Dreamflight (1989-1996)
El Rio Del Tiempo (1982-2007)
ExtraTERRORestrial Alien Encounter (1995-2003)
Flight to the Moon (1971-1975)
Food Rocks (1994-2004)
Get Happy with ABC (2002-2002)

Here Come the Muppets (1990-1991)
Honey I Shrunk the Audience (1994-2010)
Horizons (1983-1999)
Hunchback of Notre Dame: A Musical Adventure (1996-2002)
If You Could Fly (1987-1989)
If You Had Wings (1972-1987)
Journey into Imagination (1983-1998)
Journey into Jungle Book (1998-1999)
Journey into Your Imagination (1998-2002)
Kitchen Kabaret (1982-1994)
Legend of the Lion King (1994-2002)
Listen to the Land (1982-1993)
Living Seas (1986-2004)
Magic Carpet 'Round the World (1974-1975)
Magic Journeys (1982-1986; 1987-1994)
Main Street Cinema (1971-1998)
Mickey Mouse Revue (1971-1980)
Mickey's Birthdayland (1988-1990)
Mickey's Hollywood Theater (1988-1996)
Mickey's Starland (1990-1996)
Mike Fink Keel Boats (1971-1997)
Mission to Mars (1975-1993)
Monster Sound Show (1989-1997)
Mr. Toad's Wild Ride (1971-1998)
Plaza Swan Boats (1973-1983)
River Country (1976-2002)
Show Biz Is (1989-1990)
Skyway (1971-1999)
Spirit of Pocahontas (1995-1996)
Star Jets (1974-1994)
Superstar Television (1989-1999)
Symbiosis (1982-1995)
Take Flight (1989-1996)
Tarzan Rocks (1999-2006)
Timekeeper (1994-2006)
Tomorrowland Transit Authority (1994-2010)
Tomorrowland Grand Prix Raceway (1971-1996)
Treasure Island (1974-1977)

Tropical Serenade (1971-1997)
Universe of Energy (1982-1996)
Walt Disney Story (1973-1992)
WEDway PeopleMover (1975-1994)
Who Wants to be a Millionaire-Play it! (2001-2006)
Wonders of China (1982-2003)
Wonders of Life (1989-2004)
World of Motion (1982-1996)

Main Street Windows

There are enough individuals honored on Main Street to warrant a complete listing. Here they are, listed one side of the street at a time.

West Main Street (from the fire station up toward the castle)

Roger Broggie
Owen Pope
Buddy Baker
Bob Jackman
George Bruns
Ron Logan
Lonnie Lindley
Ed Bullard
Robert Jani
Charles Corson
Emile Kuri
Charlie Ridgway
Joyce Carlson
Bob Booth
Roger Broggie Jr.
John Frankie
Neil Gallagher
Jack Gladish
Rudy Pena
Dave Schweninger
Dick Van Every
Jim Verity
Morrie Houser
Lou Jennings
John Joyce
Don Edgren
John Wise
Ken Klug

Stan Maslak
John Zovich
David Snyder
Michael Bagnall
Bill Walsh
Cecil Robinson
Jack Lindquist
Dave Gengenbach
Bob Gurr
George McGinnis
Bill Watkins
Earl Vilmer
Card Walker
Ted Crowell
Arnold Lindberg
Claude Coats
Marc Davis
John DeCuir
Bill Justice
Jim Armstrong
John Curry
Howard Roland
Stan Garves
Tony Baxter
Dave Burkhart
Ed Johnson
Gary Younger
Ralph Kent

East Main Street (from the Plaza Restaurant toward Town Square)

Larry Slocum
Walt Disney
Howard Brummitt
Marvin Davis
Vic Green
John Hench
Fred Hope
Richard Irvine
Bill Martin
Chuck Myall
Bill Sullivan
Bob Matheison
Christopher Miller
Jennifer Miller
Joanna Miller
Patrick Miller
Ron and Diane Miller
Ronald Miller Jr.
Tamara Miller
Walter Miller
Don Iwerks
Ub Iwerks
Bill Washo
Bud Washo
Dick Nunis
Ron Miller
Orlando Ferrante
Abigail Disney
Roy Patrick Disney
Patty Disney
Roy E. Disney
Susan Disney
Timothy Disney
Morgan Evans
Tony Virginia
Donn Tatum

Frank Wells
Carl Bongirno
Jim McManus
Warren Robertson
Larry Tryon
Neal McClure
Dick Morrow
Spence Olin
Jim Ross
Phil Smith
Bonar Dyer
Hank Dains
Chuck Fowler
Frank Millington
Marshall Smelser
Bill Sullivan
Bob Matheison
Bob Allen
Pete Crimmings
Dick Evans
Bill Joelscher
Jack Olsen
Pete Clark
Jack Sayers
Norm Fagrell
Bud Dare
Mary Blair
Collin Campbell
Blaine Gibson
Dorothea Redmond
Herb Ryman
Nolan Browning
Roy Davis (aka Roy O. Disney)
Bob Price (aka Bob Foster)
Elias Disney

Ken Chapman
Paul Hartley
Sam McKim
Elmer Plummer
Ernie Prinzhorn
Vince Jefferds
Lou Tonarely
Wilbur Watt
Bradford Lund
Michelle Lund
Victoria Lund
William and Sharon Lund
Malcolm Cobb
Jack Ferges
Fred Joerger
Mitz Natsume
Bob Sewell
Lee Cockerell
Bruce Laval
Tom Eastman
James Passilla
Pat Vaughn
Tom Nabbe
Yale Gracey
Bud Martin
Ken O'Brien
Wathel Rogers
Bill Bosche
Jack Boyd
Bob Bigeaut

Dick Pfahler
McLaren Steward
Robert Moore
Norm Noceti
Ed Chisholm
Gordon Williams
X Atencio
Al Bertino
Marty Sklar
Doug Cayne
Joe Kramer
George Windrum
Ron Bowman
Glenn Durflinger
Don Holmquist
Dick Kline
George Nelson
Roy O. Disney
Joe Potter
Bill Irwin
Larry Reiser
Pete Markham
Dan Dingman
Francis Stanek
Bob Phelps
Ken Creekmore
Orpha Harryman
John Keehne
Alyja Paskevicius
Tom Peirce

Bonus Chapter: History at Universal Studios Florida

Islands of Adventure

- Every "island" (themed zone) of Islands of Adventure is based upon a book of some kind, such as comic books, children's books, or novels.

- The Hulk is meant to provide patrons with the "roller coaster of emotions" that results when the gamma sled experiments to restore Dr. Banner go awry.

- The tubular rails of roller coasters are usually filled with materials to dampen the noise. At the Hulk, the loud roar is intentional to match the theme, and the rails were left hollow. At Dragon Challenge, the tubes are filled with peat gravel to provide the aural sensation of animalistic flight.

- When first built, the linear induction motors (LIM) that provide the launch to the Hulk generated such a strong magnetic field that any credit cards brought on board by riders were demagnetized. Since that would have ruined the day at the park, this had to be redesigned before opening.

- The delay riders experience on the lift of the Hulk is actually time used to weigh the car, so a computer can decide the amount of thrust needed. A heavier car will be accelerated faster; up to 60 MPH in just 1.8 seconds.

- Another Marvel superhero lurks in Spider-Man: Iron Man shows up two times in the Spider-Man ride—he can be seen in the first room with a 3-D screen, painted near the top of a building, and he is visible again near the end of the ride, as our vehicle is being dragged around. Watch the bottom-right of the screen for an advertisement from Stark Industries that includes Iron Man.

- A phone number visible in the Spider-Man ride is an actual phone line maintained by Universal Studios, just to reward sharp-eyed visitors with cell phones. Right before our ascent into the skyscrapers during the final scenes of the ride, Spider-Man clings to a theater's marquee, on which a phone number is visible. If visitors later call the displayed numbers, 407-224-1783, they will hear this recorded message: "Thank you for calling the Coup Theater. Due to the recent unpleasantness caused by Doc Ock and his gang of villains, we will be closed until further notice… or at least until Spider-Man can make our city safe again. Beep!" This phone number once belonged to Thierry Coup, the creative director for the Spider-Man attraction. The name of the theater is a further tribute to Coup.

- An oversized sandstone wall along the major pathway in Jurassic Park, near to the Discovery Center, blocks a smaller walkway that once led to an attraction called Triceratops Encounter. Park visitors would be ushered into a small room where a full-sized triceratops rested sedately within reach. This robotic performer wiggled, blinked, snorted, and moved in many small ways to convey the sense of reality. To commemorate the extinct attraction, which closed in 2004, designers inscribed the sandstone blocking the walkway with triceratops bones.

- A boat dock in Jurassic Park's waterside jungles is a remnant of a former attraction called Island Skipper Tours, which used to transport visitors across the lagoon near to the park's entrance. To save patrons the trouble of walking the half-circle needed to exit the park (or that same distance at the start of the day), boats were used to make the journey more quickly. They closed in 2002.

- A representation of Dr. Seuss himself can be seen in Seuss Landing. Just opposite the entrance to the High in the Sky Trolley is a photo location with a statue of a policeman; just above that are three mayoral figures carved on the wall. The one on the left, wearing glasses, sports the visage of Theodor Geisel, the real-life author (1904-1991) whose pseudonym was Dr. Seuss.

- The buildings in Seuss Landing are made from Styrofoam. For proof of the strange heritage in its building materials, simply knock on any wall with your knuckles, and it should sound hollow. The rounded look of the buildings was accomplished by using chain saws to individually sculpt every façade.

- The High in the Sky Seuss Trolley Train Ride may have opened in 2006, but the track had sat empty since 1999 because the original concept, individual cars called "Sylvester McMonkey McBean's Very Unusual Driving Machines," could not be built due to safety concerns.

Universal Studios Florida

- Mouse Ears on the tires of a car at Twister provide a tongue-in-cheek reference to Orlando's other big theme park operator. In the queue of Twister, a car dangles from the ceiling, with one wheel still spinning as if disaster has just occurred. On that tire is a familiar hat with Mouse Ears, as if implying the car had run over someone who had visited the competition!

- The sounds of the tornado in Twister were not merely recorded from a live storm. Rather, designers took the sounds of animals and contorted them. Incongruously, to get the sound we now hear, they mixed the howls of a lion, a camel, and a monkey, stretched the mixture, and played it backwards.

- The exit doors of Twister are vacuum sealed. This is not by design; it's an unintentional by-product of all the pressure that builds up inside the attraction each time it operates.

- The funnel cloud in Twister is a real vortex, not an optical illusion or special effect. The barometric pressure of the outside weather plays a role as well. On days with poor weather and low pressure, the vortex inside the attraction will be thicker.

- The New York streets are a direct result of director Steven Spielberg's experiences as a young man in Universal Studios-Hollywood. When he was an aspiring filmmaker, Spielberg took the standard tourist tram tour in the Hollywood park, but he was disillusioned that the tram didn't actually see any filming going on. So he snuck off the tram tour and set out on his own, eventually camping out in an unused bungalow and essentially squatting on the Universal property. Though several insiders knew what he was up to, they allowed him to stay, and soon enough

Spielberg had real movies (and instant hits) to his name, and his presence became legitimate. When he was tapped to help design the Orlando park, Spielberg remembered the problem of a tram tour where the filming action took place in the "back lot," so he increased the likelihood of tourists seeing filming by building those sets in the "front lot," right at the theme park, in the first place.

- The New York streets reproduce several famous facades from movies. The Empire Hotel is from *Vertigo*, the café is from *Batteries Not Included*, and there are facades from *Annie*, *The Sting*, and *West Side Story* as well.

- The former occupant of the building which now houses the Mummy is commemorated inside the Mummy's treasure room. Since King Kong was originally the ride taking up this space, designers included a two-foot tall golden statue of Kong in this room. Look for it on the left side, just past the halfway point in the room, high up near the ceiling.

- The hieroglyphics on the walls of the queue use authentic symbols and warn of Imhotep. The hieroglyphics in the treasure room are also authentic, but these pay further homage to King Kong, with phrases such as "Kong is watching you" and "Kong will never die." There are also hieroglyphics that provide directions to the Mummy coaster's control booth.

- When King Kong was present in the park, an artificial odor was pumped into the room where park visitors came face to face with him. Universal even trademarked this scent, which went by the name of Banana Breath. Other Universal-trademarked odors include Burnt Shark (used at the Jaws ride) and Musty Forest (used at the E.T. attraction).

- The "fake ending" of the Mummy, where the ride attendant is seemingly killed in front of us, was a gag originally written for a Stephen King ride that never came to fruition.

The idea was kept around at Universal Creative, the arm of the company that designs theme parks, in keeping with a philosophy of not throwing any good idea away and recycling them when possible into other projects.

- The predecessor to Disaster! was simply called Earthquake, and the new Disaster! attraction keeps the focus in the finale on the temblor. Although the new attraction focuses on different kinds of disasters, the final scene was left intact from the original ride, so visitors only experience an earthquake and its related effects, such as fire and flood.

- The original ending of the Jaws ride made use of an exploding shark, whose pieces were gathered up by a net and re-assembled every few minutes like a giant jigsaw. The effect was difficult to maintain and suffered maintenance nightmares, and was eventually replaced by the current shark, which does not explode into pieces.

- Men in Black is designed to look like a World's Fair exhibit but function in reality as a training facility for the alien-fighting program. Only three endings were written for Will Smith to record, but in the studio he improvised over fifty different endings for the ride. It takes exotic situations, like really diverse results between the two cars, to hear the unusual recordings. The pithy comments when a team scores especially low include "you zigged when you should have zagged" and "the Men in PINK is right down the street."

- Look for Steven Spielberg himself, the maestro behind the Florida version of the Universal Studios park, to be represented as a cardboard cutout on a bus in the first training portion of Men in Black.

- The Simpsons Ride honors the former occupant of this space, the Back to the Future Ride, in a multiple ways in the queue. Christopher Lloyd, the actor who portrayed Doc

Emmett Brown in the Back to the Future movies, lent his voice to a cartoon version of himself that plays briefly on the overhead monitors. In this skit, Professor Frink (the scientist on the Simpsons) goes to visit the Institute of Future Technology and sees instead the same Krustyland façade we passed through a minute ago. Depressed, he realizes he can't see Doc Brown, his hero... unless he travels back in time with a Delorean. He hops in one conveniently nearby, and zooms back two years ago. As he materializes, he runs over a man next to Doc Brown. Turns out Doc Brown was about to sign a contract for a small business loan, which would enable him to keep the Institute of Future Technology open. So Professor Frink has actually caused Doc Brown to go out of business! Krusty shows up, and promptly hires Doc Brown as a ticket-taker for his new park, since Krusty is going to own the land.

- The really sharp visitors can also hear a quick reminder of the Back to the Future experience. Originally, Doc told us just before we boarded the cars that the psychopath Biff Tannen was running loose in the facility. In the Simpsons Ride, Krusty says much the same thing about Sideshow Bob and a psychopath loose in the area.

- The Simpsons Ride itself also pays homage to Back to the Future. In the original Back to the Future Ride, a dinosaur ate our vehicle in a distinctive one-two swallowing motion before our escape, and this is repeated by giant Maggie attempting to use our car as a pacifier. Not coincidentally, this is occurring at an outdoor square in Springfield that ought to look familiar; it's a cartoon version of the famous square and courthouse from Back to the Future (you can see the clock tower clearly).

- E.T. the Extra-Terrestrial Adventure is the last original ride in Universal Studios Florida, which opened in 1989 (Jaws, though it opened that same year, has been significantly changed).

- The cityscape model we fly over in E.T. was built in Atlanta and designed to break apart into three parts so it could fit through the large hangar doors of the attraction, but when it arrived, it still wouldn't fit, so the entire model had to be painstakingly disassembled and reassembled after all, a process that took an additional three months.

- Except for the building housing Terminator 2: 3-D Battle Across Time, all the facades in the area were inspired by real buildings in Hollywood. The villas at the end of the street are reproductions of the famous hotel that was the first ever to feature private bathrooms, and had been owned by a silent film actress. Until the Terminator attraction was opened in 1996, the street was home to a sedate tram tour that navigated the park right in the same area as tourists walked.

- The empty building and soundstage across from Mel's Drive-In was once home to multiple shows. First used for Murder She Wrote (which provided an explanation of Foley artists and the sound work that goes into film), it would later house shows based on Hercules and Xena.

- The theater housing Shrek 4-D was once home to Alfred Hitchcock Presents, a celebration of moviemaking by the famous Hollywood director. With Shrek, the theater took on a decidedly more snarky tone. Faux movie posters in the queue, for instance, poke fun at Disney park attractions such as Dumbo the flying elephant.

- The Jimmy Neutron ride was once used for a Hanna-Barbera motion simulator. The new ride pays homage to virtually all of the Nickelodeon characters in a quick montage at the start of the film. The movie also nods to its fellow attraction up the road (T2: 3D) by showing us an alien planet with a movie theater, on whose marquee we see "E2, Starring Arnold Schwarzenegger."

Afterword

Every year about thirty million people visit Walt Disney World, making it one of the top tourist destinations in the United States. Disney built its theme parks in the middle of nowhere, and still the people descended in droves. The number of visitors is possibly a better choice than any other tidbit to encapsulate the message of this book: people will come in record numbers to experience the magic Disney produces, and central to the Disney magic are these details and tributes, a combined reverence for the past and for historical accuracy. Those details create the "Disney Difference" which draws people and keeps them coming back for more every year.

While many patrons consciously think only about the rides at Walt Disney World, it's the rich sub-culture of homages, tributes, fun details, intricate trivia, and rich backstories at the parks which do the heavy lifting of enchanting our imaginations.

The Disney attention to detail is legendary, and rightly so. Only by exposing the level to which these details are researched, sought after, refined, and finally implemented can we begin to understand the richness of the tapestry at a Disney theme park. The persuasive tricking of our senses, the completely believable immersion into fictitious realms, and the unconditional suspension of disbelief all owe their existence to such details that seem, at first glance, to be mere adornments, or perhaps even indulgences by the artists.

Don't be fooled. It's the details at Disney that render the experience magical. To know the details is to examine the magician's trick hat— you will have a fuller understanding of what's going on and what to watch for, and it will only increase your enjoyment of the effect.

Kevin Yee

About the Author

Kevin Yee spent more than a decade working at Disneyland and cultivating a never-ending fascination with that park's rich traditions and history. Now relocated to Orlando, Kevin has visited the Walt Disney World parks more than 600 times. He also enjoys traveling to the Disney parks in other countries.

Kevin is the author of several Disney books:

- *Mouse Trap: Memoir of a Disneyland Cast Member.* This affectionate recounting of fifteen years of working for Disneyland on the front lines provides an inside glimpse at life working for the Mouse, including its perks and its rewards, and allows those on the outside to imagine what life is like on the inside of the "trap."
- *Tokyo Disney Made Easy.* This guide to Tokyo Disneyland and Tokyo DisneySea takes all the guesswork out of a journey to Japan and the phenomenal Disney parks there. You'll have step by step guidelines for what to do and what to expect, so there is no worry whatsoever on your visit, even if you don't speak a word of Japanese.
- *Magic Quizdom.* A trivia book dedicated only to Disneyland, this book specializes in historical items and dates for Walt's original Magic Kingdom.
- *101 Things You Never Knew About Disneyland.* Hidden history and insider tributes abound at Disneyland, and this book charts all of them, to make your visit to Disneyland all the more magical by reveling in the history all around you.

These works can be ordered from online bookseller Amazon.com.

An online journalist and columnist since 1997, Kevin now publishes at MiceAge.com, UltimateOrlando.com, and TheDisneyBlog.com.

Index

Made in the USA
Lexington, KY
12 December 2011